Making and Planning a Small Garden

Other Concorde Books

Making and Planning a Small Garden

Edited by
Roger Grounds

WARD LOCK LIMITED · LONDON

First published in Great Britain in 1973
by Ward Lock Limited, 116 Baker Street,
London, W1M 2BB

Text in Baskerville (169/312)

Printed Offset Litho and bound by
Cox & Wyman Ltd
London, Fakenham and Reading

Contents

Introduction

Making a garden can always be fun and should never be hard work. There's ·certainly more fun in making a garden than in maintaining one. And good gardens don't just happen – they're planned. And you don't need to be a chartered surveyor to do that, any more than you need to be an architect to plan the living-room.

All you need are some sample plans to show you how it is done, a pinch of imagination to blend the various elements together to make a plan to suit your particular garden, and a little elementary know-how to carry it out. And that's precisely what this book provides you with: all the information you need to plan and create a garden that will be not only a joy to you but also a considerable asset to your property.

1 The Modern Garden

There has never been such an exciting time for gardeners. The modern garden is the outcome of centuries of evolution and development. All that is best from the past has been kept, all that is least acceptable to modern ideas discarded. Gardens may not be so large as they were in the past but they are vastly richer in the means both to make them more beautiful and easier to maintain.

The gardens of England and New England, of Canberra and San Francisco have been enriched not only by the treasures brought back by the brave plant hunters of the early years of this century from the rain forests of the Andes and the slopes of the Himalayas, from the cold clime of Kamchatka and from sunny South Africa, but also by the highly skilled labours of hybridizers. There has never, at any time in the past, been such a wealth of plants from which to create colourful and fruitful gardens. Precisely the same is true of garden design, where not only can one draw on the best ideas of the great traditions of Europe and America, but also on those of such countries as Japan.

All gardeners must be influenced by the past which lives on in the gardens of great country houses and to a large extent in public parks, and do their best to marry the traditional with the taste and requirements of today. To this end there are aids available of which our forebears never dreamed. And those who supply us with plants and seeds will tell us that we have an ever-increasing appetite for novelty and improvement in all kinds of garden plants!

The gardener, too, has changed with the times. If we were to seek today's typical gardener we would find him or her looking after a suburban 'front and back' in which up to two-thirds of the area is devoted to lawn, and the rest mainly to flowers, roses, flowering shrubs and possibly some vegetables. Our gardener will be equipped with an armoury of aids, some traditional, others very modern.

Elements of the Modern Garden. So let us look more closely at the components of a pleasing and useful garden. There is no set formula, but some features are common to most gardens. A garden without flowers is unthinkable, at least for the area that can be seen from the house. And until recently the design was not complete without a lawn – often two. Today, however, paving and other hard surfaces are no longer restricted to paths and service areas.

Imaginative use is being made of pre-formed slabs, cobbles granite setts or chippings as labour-saving groundwork, relieved by formal beds and perhaps a fish pool or statue. Such modern garden design is particularly appropriate in the context of the 'town house' terrace. This architectural approach has brought with it a new interest in the form and texture of plants, which accounts for the growing sales by nurseries and garden centres of miniature evergreens and compact shrubs with grey, silver and variegated foliage.

However, for the majority a green lawn remains the perfect restful foil, with improved machines to take the toil out of mowing – and there are even powered edging machines to give that clean finish without any effort. The balance of herbaceous border flowers, bedding plants and bulbs depends so much on personal preference – though most of us will pack in as many of each as space, time and ready cash allow. Selection and management of these flowers is covered in later sections. Flowers need no general words of commendation, but it can be said that flowering shrubs still remain relatively neglected, while ornamental trees come lower still in the garden-makers' list of priorities.

It is true, of course, that for a couple of weeks in spring gardens are gay with golden-yellow forsythia, pink cherry, berberis and the very modest mauve of ribes – followed very much later by an autumn blaze of berries from cotoneaster and pyrancantha. But this is just a scratch at the surface. The rose is regarded as a shrub and is justly a firm favourite. Yet it is so easy to be wooed by those who wish to sell only hybrid teas and floribundas, to the exclusion of the informal beauty of the shrub roses and the delightful older varieties that clothe walls, fences, arches and doorways so well.

Generally speaking shrubs will look after themselves if kept in proportion by restrained use of secateurs. Fruit trees are ornamental as well as productive. Newcomers to gardening tend to avoid them, but those grown for garden planting today are nearly all raised on rootstocks that impart a dwarf habit and slow growth so there is little fear that they will get out of hand. Bush fruit is easy to manage and the new gardener is well advised to plant some of the types that rarely appear in fruit shops today – such as red and white currants. They will not take up much space, while a row of raspberries can make a useful and quite attractive screen between 'kitchen' and 'pleasure' areas.

Vegetable gardening has cast off its gloomy, cloth-cap war-time image and become an interesting and rewarding pastime. So consider allocating an area to a rotation of 'salads', 'roots' and 'greens'. Lady gardeners need no persuasion to grow herbs, which are charming in growth and piquant in the pot: it's best to allocate them a special bed near the kitchen or even to maintain them on the windowsill in posts or a box.

Soil, Site and Climate. Any gardener must be a realist and respect the limitations of his site while, at the same time, using all his resources to overcome problems. For example, on a windswept hillside there will be constant damage to all but the lowest growing plants until a screen is provided to filter the prevailing wind. This may be in the form of a lattice fence, hedge or group of trees – and must be considered a priority. Disappointment will be inevitable if the gardener insists on trying to grow the more tender shrubs in exposed northern districts, just as extremes of dryness in a sunny situation or shade cast by

Instant Garden. Any garden can be made as attractive as this almost instantly — within months of moving into a house. The lawn is turfed and most of the colour is provided by bedding plants.

buildings or trees will limit the growth of a wider range of plants.

Other considerations are the size, shape and slope of the site. A little, but not much, can be done to counter the influence of local topography and climate on the garden, but the native soil is another matter altogether. Its type will certainly influence the character of the garden, but no gardener worth his salt will admit defeat because he is presented in the first place with inhospitable clay, sand or chalk. The degree of acidity or alkalinity will influence what can be grown – in a lime-rich soil the rhododendron tribe will never be happy and hydrangeas will be pink rather than blue. Slight acidity suits the majority of garden plants, while the inclusion of peat, organic matter from compost heaps, animal manure and acidic fertilizers will all ameliorate excess alkalinity.

The pleasant task of garden-making always begins on paper – graph paper – on which a scale plan is drawn. The larger the paper, the easier and more accurate the draughtsmanship. Start by measuring the outside perimeter of the house and then choose a scale that will enable the whole site area to fit on paper: four or eight foot to the inch is often employed. Some rudimentary surveying equipment is required, the basics being a stout tape measure, a couple of long lines of cord, nylon or wire, half a dozen stout pointed stakes about a foot long, an equal number of 4-ft. bamboo canes, and a large right-angle triangle made of wood. Take as a base line a wall of the house that faces the greatest part of the garden and run lines at right angles from this wall until they meet the boundary of the site. If the line of sight is impeded, set up canes along the line so that each is exactly in front of the previous one when viewed with the eye close to it. Transfer these maximum distances to the graph paper, marking the boundary points with dots.

From points along these initial lines (marked by canes) run 'branches' at right angles until these lines reach other garden boundaries. Measure the distances and transfer them to the plan. If the garden is on several sides of the house, these house walls must be used as new base lines to make further right angle measurements. When sufficient dots have been made on the paper they can be joined up to make an accurate perimeter plan of the site. Also measure and mark the position of any tree or other permanent feature that is to be retained.

Draughtsman's tracing paper now comes in useful. Pin a sheet over the graph paper and sketch in possible positions for certain major features – paths, borders, lawn, 'kitchen' area, pool, greenhouse and so on. Over this can be placed another sheet of tracing paper on which variations and other details can be marked in a different colour. In this way a picture of the future garden can be built up and changed until the ideal is achieved. Aim for simplicity and seek a balance between straight lines (as for paths) and sweeping curves (for lawn and border edges). Bear in mind that an 'artistic' design of little beds in grass or winding paths may look nice on paper but that to translate it into spade-work and concrete mixing can be a herculean task at the outset and require constant edging and maintenance. Rather allow for a larger lawn area than you might think you want, and include a large sweeping border instead of scattered beds. Later it will be much easier to cut into the grass area to make another feature (or put additional shrubs in a big border) than to erase items from an over-fussy or time-consuming layout.

While still at the planning stage, some design principles should be noted. To create an effect of greater distance make a focal point, with a tree, sundial or seat for example, at the end of a converging vista, and let a path 'disappear' behind an external hedge or trellis. Conversely, to shorten a long site divide the garden into self-contained areas. For example, a circular lawn near the house with a low hollow wall on its far side will concentrate interest on its pleasing proportions so that the eye is less distracted by the length of garden beyond. Most garden perimeters are rectangular, so try to break the rectangle by curving the edges of lawn and borders.

Above all be realistic: design for easy management. Have good access paths for the mower and other heavy tools; this may mean a slope instead of steps. Consider bringing the food-growing area and greenhouse near the dwelling house if ease of access is more important than eye-appeal. Remember that you may want to supply electricity to the greenhouse, or even have a heated frame and that it is pointless to place a shed at the bottom

Another informal pond. This one has been created with modern plastic sheeting. The paving round the edge holds the sheeting in place.

14

Here a rock garden has been used to add interest to a garden that would otherwise have been completely flat. It has turned a boring suburban plot into a charming garden.

of the plot and tramp the whole distance for every item that is kept there.

Ground-work. If the garden is on level land there should be no need to move soil in any quantity unless it is to relieve uniform flatness by creating undulations. An artificial mound must often be raised for a rock garden and it can be an economy to plant this in combination with a pool: the excavation for one making the elevation for the other.

On a site where the main garden falls away from the house a primary task could be to make a terrace against the house for which purpose the ground requires building up. The fall of a site can be broken at any point by raising a low wall of stone or brick, moving some soil to the higher level at the same time, and interrupting the wall with a couple of steps. Gardens which slope towards the house clearly present drainage problems. But if the nature of the site demands such an arrangement, strong banking will be needed with seep-holes through which surplus water can flow to drains linked with the domestic system.

For the lawn a level site is generally preferable though a slight slope will assist drainage and lawn management. Some soil movement is generally necessary, and a cardinal rule is to preserve the valuable top soil which may get turned during excavation. So shovel away as much top soil as is practicable from the area of soil movement, and keep it heaped near by.

A slope can be levelled in three ways: (1) by adopting the lowest level and removing all soil above this; (2) by adopting the highest level and importing soil; (3) by choosing the intermediate level and removing high ground to fill low ground. Unless dramatic changes in level are required, the third alternative is the one requiring least effort and soil upset.

Here is one way to level a site. Cultivate the ground roughly and move soil (with the precaution of reserving top-soil) until the site is roughly level by eye. Final adjustments are made with the aid of pegs, a mallet, a plank about 6 ft. long and a spirit-level. At a central spot in the area being levelled knock in a peg until it is flush with the ground. Knock in another peg the same distance from the first one as the length of the plank, and adjust it until the plank spanning the two pegs is level according to the spirit-level placed on top. The second peg may then be proud of the ground or slightly sunk, so soil must be added or removed accordingly. Proceed in this way across the site moving soil with a rake. Finally replace any reserved top soil and distribute evenly.

While still at the early design and soil moving stage, the gardener is strongly advised to investigate whether artificial drainage is required. Free percolation of excess rainwater from the region of plant roots is a prerequisite of healthy growth. A light sandy soil will have no problems in this respect: indeed it may require the addition of water-holding organic matter. But even a light surface soil can have its drainage impeded by an impervious lower layer. A heavy clay soil will inevitably be slow to drain. Puddles that remain on the surface after rain constitute a drainage problem.

Be resolute and put in drainage channels at an early stage. No one will deny that it is hard work, but it may make the difference between pleasure and dismay in future gardening activities. To conduct water there must be a gradient. If the garden slopes, then take advantage of this to run channels to a ditch or 'soakaway' at the lowest point. On a level site, the channels themselves must cut more deeply into the ground as they cross the site to the chosen outflow point. Remember that standing water can be useful in the right place: a low-lying area can make an excellent bog garden.

Normally, drainage water should be discharged into an existing ditch or into a rubble-filled soakaway which is dug as deeply as possible at the lowest point. Agricultural land drains are the most permanent, laid end to end in a narrow trench about 2 ft. deep and surrounded with 3 in. of clinker or rubble. The alternative is to dig a similar trench and pack it with 9-in. depth of graded rubble in place of pipe drains. A single drain across the site is rarely sufficient, and a herring-bone pattern of branches, say 15 ft. apart, falling to meet the main drain should ensure adequate drainage on the most difficult land.

Soils and What to Make of Them. To discover the main constituents of a soil, all that is required is an empty milk bottle. Dig a narrow hole with a trowel and remove a slice from the side to a depth of 3–4 in. Crumble this into the milk bottle. Pour in water to cover the soil and shake the contents well.

▲ Two of the most popular roses raised this century, 'Elizabeth of Glamis' and 'Fragrant Cloud'.

Irises are amongst the easiest of all border plants, invariably putting up a good show and needing little attention.

Every garden needs some sort of feature to draw the eye. A sundial ▶ is one such traditional feature

A typical pre-war house can be made really charming with some ▶ climbing plants, a rockery, and a small pond.

18

When this is left to settle, the heavier constituents will fall to the bottom first and the lighter parts will form narrow bands above. This will give an indication of the proportions of grit, sand, silt, clay and organic matter present. Generally speaking, the coarser the particle size the easier will be the management of the soil.

Simply by sight and touch you can ascertain if a lump of soil sticks and smears (clay); has a fine gritty texture (silt or fine sand); or crumbles into smaller soil particles (loam). Best of all is old meadow land where root penetration by grasses, the manure of animals and the activity of earth-worms have created a deep, crumbly fibrous loam.

Chemical soil analysis is best carried out with the help of a soil test kit which can be purchased from any garden sundries supplier. First stage testing is for acidity or alkalinity. This is generally done by shaking a sample of soil in water and dipping specially treated paper strips into the solution. The colour which the strip adopts is then compared with a chart showing degree of acidity or alkalinity. An extreme of either will be problematic – but is not often found. A neutral or slightly acidic reaction is a happy state of affairs for general purpose gardening.

More sophisticated soil test kits enable the plant foods present to be analysed. Gardeners should also know that every county has its horticultural officer, usually attached to a training college or institute, who is able to get a sample of soil analysed for the private gardener. We have now opened the door to the complex and controversial world of the soil and the additions that man incorporates.

There are three major plant foods – nitrogen, potash and phosphate – commonly symbolized as N, K and P. An analysis on a fertilizer package may show the symbols K_2O and P_2O_5 which are merely the 'full' food value symbols. As well as these there are several minor but essential elements needed by plants, such as calcium, iron, magnesium, manganese, boron. Sufficient of these occur in most properly managed soils. Nitrogen encourages green growth while the others play vital roles in making roots, strong stems, swelling fruit or giving flower colour.

Under natural conditions there is a cycle by which plants and animals contribute their debris to the soil. This debris is rich in plant food as well as being organic material that improves the structure and health of the soil during its decay into humus.

When man cultivates a garden he inevitably interrupts this natural cycle and makes great demands on the food reserve of the soil. He will tend, for example, to keep ground bare around clumps of flowers and shrubs so that little vegetation returns below ground. He will try to grow several crops of salads or other vegetables from the same site in a year, and remove grass clippings when the lawn is mown.

It does not take long for the ground to become hungry, and when it does, the quality of garden plants deteriorates. The best way to repay the debt to the soil is always to add farmyard manure, which contains all the plant foods together with straw for improving structure. The next best thing is properly rotted plant and kitchen waste, which we call compost (not to be confused with sowing and potting compost). Useful additional soil improvement comes from upturning and burying a carpet of annual weeds during the course of a year. But this natural feeding is not enough for an intensively cultivated garden, and concentrated N, P and K should be provided by modest applications of artificial fertilizer. Additional calcium comes from scattering lime (but only if the soil is neutral or acid). Peat has no food value but improves structure and makes soil less alkaline.

Lime is also scattered on heavy land to assist its breakdown. The transformation of heavy clay into friable loam is the dream of all gardeners unlucky enough to be stuck with the former, and in recent years a range of 'miracle' products has been offered as a cure. They will do what is promised of them – but in time, and at a price. Another material for the same job is gypsum, which has been known and used far longer than the alginates, of which most of the clay-breaking products are composed.

The natural way of creating a surface tilth is through the combined effects of winter freezing and thawing which shatter lumps into ever smaller pieces, and by the drying effect of winds which continues the crumbling process. This is true of all soils that form clods when wet, and the gardener should not be anxious to break these down when he carries out autumn digging after clearance of summer flowers and vegetables.

It cannot be over-emphasized how vital is the addition of decaying organic matter to the soil for the health of the garden and its easier management. The effect is cumulative. The humus so provided enriches the soil and also 'opens it up', so that water and air pass more freely. Thus it dries and warms up more quickly in the spring, and growth is not delayed. Organic matter attracts earthworms which help to bury it, and by their burrowings they aerate and drain the soil further. Such a soil will have a balanced ecology.

Friend or Foe. A word about friends and foes in the garden – especially foes, which can be combated with a great array of chemical weapons these days. The foes you face are the insects who wish to share the fruits of your endeavours (there are also larger creatures such as birds and mice which are not being considered here); fungal spores which alight and develop on our plants when conditions are right for them, and weeds. Friends occur in the insect camp, notably among the ladybirds and parasitic wasps, and in the soil are found the helpful centipede (which is more active than the harmful millipede), certain burying beetles and the invaluable earthworm. Any damage done by birds is compensated by their activity in searching out pests, including slugs and snails.

Before resorting to chemical controls, be sure that other approaches have been tried. There is no substitute for good hygiene in the garden. This concerns such points as removing all trash and litter for composting or burning, avoiding dense, damp tangles of growth which are breeding grounds for pests and diseases. It means attending to hand weeding, cutting back dead growth, digging out the last remains of food crops – and keeping tools clean. Its attention to detail, for which there is another phrase – green fingers. But when troubles are rife, as will be the case from time to time in every garden, then go in with modern aids and apply the knock-out before epidemic levels develop. Even so, don't get carried away just because a suitable spray is to hand. It may be just as easy, cheaper and at nil risk to the environment if, say, a few greenfly are squeezed between finger and thumb, some caterpillars picked off by hand, or a patch of weeds pulled out of the lawn rather than spot-sprayed.

Protection and prevention is obviously wiser than last-minute action to combat a big build-up of trouble. There are pesticides (insect-killers) with limited persistence in the plant's sap stream

An informal series of ponds in a medium-sized garden. The plant in the middle is *Gunnera manicata*. You grow it at your peril: the leaves can be up to 6ft across.

so that pests arriving the day after spraying will be controlled. These sprays are called systemic. The same property will soon be introduced into fungicides but in the meantime these materials are best sprayed on to susceptible foliage, such as that of the rose, ahead of possible infection so that a protective barrier is formed.

The technical word for weedkiller is herbicide and here too there are innovations of great value. The sooner gardeners forget about that dangerous total growth killer sodium chlorate, the better. There are other 'total' materials which have no fire risk and which allow the ground to be sown or planted quite quickly afterwards. There are selective herbicides for use on the lawn which will destroy broad-leafed weeds but which leave grasses unaffected. And there are newer ones which if sprayed on clean ground among woody plants prevent fresh weed growth.

2 Techniques of Gardening

Surveying the Site. The very first thing to do with any garden is to survey it. This is not a difficult operation: you do not need to be a chartered surveyor, nor do you need complicated instruments. Basically all you need to do initially is walk round your garden and determine what you want to do with it, and what the problems are going to be. You will need to take reasonably accurate measurements of the dimensions of the garden, so that you can draw up accurate plans.

In the garden of a newly built house there is usually little difficulty in doing this. However, if you have bought an old house with an established garden the problems may be rather different. Established gardens are basically of two types: those that have been maintained in good order, and those that have been neglected. If you take on an established garden that has been maintained in good order the wisest thing to do is simply to carry on maintaining it in good order for your first year: this will enable you to find out what is already in the garden, before deciding to make any changes. If, however, you have taken on a neglected garden you will have a lot of clearance work to do before you can survey the site: indeed, you may have quite a lot to do before you can even establish the true boundaries.

Site Clearance. Clearing the site is an essential operation in all gardens, old and new, but the problems of each are different.

With old, overgrown gardens the first thing to do is to clear away the overgrowth: only when this has been done can you establish the boundaries and the lie of the land. The simplest way of clearing the overgrowth is to hire a mechanical scythe, mow down all perennial growths, and then to take saw or secateurs to any scrubby growth.

With old gardens that are merely in need of renovating, and in which you are not planning to undertake any major earth-moving or construction work, the next step is the removal of a number of weeds which may have become well established, such as ground-elder. The simplest and most efficient way of attacking this task is to hire a flame-thrower. A word of warning however: they are not the easiest of tools to use and can be dangerous unless handled with care and forethought. They are definitely not suitable for use by women. After burning the ground the surface of the soil should then be broken up, and this is best done with a mechanical rotovator – another tool that can easily be hired. These, again, are not tools for women to use, and they are rather inclined to run away with anyone not prepared to control them with a strong hand. Where trees need to be removed the branches should first be sawn off, leaving a stem about 3 ft. high: the top of this should be drilled with a deep hole, and into the hole should be poured a proprietary tree-killing chemical: it is important to follow the maker's instructions implicitly: too much of the chemical will kill only the top growth, not the roots, while too little will also have precisely the same effect. In a couple of years the dead stump will be quite easy to remove. Meanwhile it can be covered with a clematis or turned into a bird-table.

The problems that face those who have taken on a garden surrounding a newly built house are rather different. In the first place it is quite possible that the builder will have removed all your top-soil and left you with only the relatively infertile and intractable sub-soil: in which case you will have to buy back the top-soil from him, usually at considerable cost. The top-soil should not, however, be brought back into the garden until all levelling and changes of level have been made. Apart from this, where patios, paths and drives are to be made no top-soil will be needed, so it is a waste of time and effort to replace it only to have to remove it all again.

Even if the builder has had the kindness to leave your garden with its original top-soil, the chances are that he will also have left you with quite a number of other things – such as broken bricks, large slabs of concrete, broken milk-bottles: you may also find that he has buried pieces of corrugated iron, roofing felt, sheets of plastic and other substances incompatible with fertility and good drainage.

These should all be removed. Where large slabs of concrete occur – as they often do where the site concrete mixer has been standing, these must be broken up with a sledge hammer, or levered out of the ground with a crow-bar or pick-axe. The concrete rubble is worth retaining somewhere on the site if you are contemplating laying a drive, paths or a patio: it will save having to buy in hardcore.

Soil. To the non-gardener earth is just earth. It is when you want to start growing things in it that it begins to take on a rather different character.

Soil is made up of two basic types of material – mineral and organic. The mineral part is the result of vast geological forces that have, with the assistance of weathering over an immense period of time, broken down basic rocks into finer and finer particles. Basically therefore, the type of soil in any garden will depend very largely upon the type of rock from which it has been broken down. The organic part of earth is what is called humus. Humus is the sum of all the decaying vegetable and animal matter in the soil. What it does is to form within the structure of the soil a kind of sponge which retains water and enables plants to acquire essential nutrients from the soil.

There is a third component of soils that is often forgotten: and that is what is known as the soil population. This is made up of a surprisingly large number of creatures, some of them beneficial, others pestilential, which live in the soil: these include not only the obvious creature, such as earthworms, but also a very large number of micro-organisms. The extent of the soil population will depend largely upon the amount of humus in the soil: it is the function of these micro-organisms to break down dead creatures and vegetation and release the plant nutrients locked up in them so that the plants can use them. Thus the overall fertility of any soil depends upon the ratios in which these various elements are combined.

Gardeners recognize a number of different types of soil: each has its own peculiar advantages and disadvantages.

Basic Soil Types

LOAM. This is the ideal soil in relation to structure. It feels smooth without being gritty or sticky rubbed in the hand when sampled moist. Neither is it powdery. A light loam has more sand in it – more than two-thirds. A heavy loam has more clay – more than one-third. A medium loam has just the right texture and retains water and food well. It warms up quickly in spring, enabling plants to get away to a good start. If it becomes very acid it will need dressings of lime, and it is best to add small amounts of lime at regular intervals rather than wait till the soil becomes too acid. Humus-making composts and manures will be needed, as well as fertilizers.

SAND. This is a non-sticky soil even when wet, and those used to heavy soils often envy gardeners with sandy soils because the latter are so easy to dig or hoe. But it is a hungry soil needing a lot of manure, peat, compost, etc. and fertilizers. It warms up quickly in spring for early sowings.

CLAY. A heavy, cold soil, it is sticky to the touch when wet and binds up into unbreakable lumps in dry weather. Improvement of drainage as mentioned will help it to release the valuable plant foods usually retained in clay. These will also need supplementing with fertilizers. It is usually too acid and more liberal liming will be needed than on loam.

CHALK. These soils are rich in lime and so one cannot grow lime-hating plants such as heathers and rhododendrons. The top-soil is often dark and thin exposing a white or light coloured sub-soil of almost pure chalk. The ground seems very wet and sticky after it has rained, rather like clay, but it then dries out rapidly, becoming hard and rough to the touch. It is more easily and profitably dug in this state. There is a great need to improve it with organic humus-making matter including strawy manure, compost, peat, etc., in order to help it retain the moisture better. Avoid deep digging or you will bring up the sub-soil, which is a fatal thing to do. Mulching helps to retain moisture and dressings of lime may become necessary from time to time.

PEAT. Dark, spongy soil often very rich in plant foods, if it is the fen peat type, it will need good drainage and lime, as it is invariably too acid. Peat soils should not be over-limed, however, as this upsets the chemical balance of the soil.

STONY. The proverbial infertility of stony ground is due to the fact that all the moisture runs out of it quickly. However, a few stones in the soil may actually help to retain the moisture. It is, in any case, an almost impossible task to remove all the stones as more seem to surface to take the place of those removed. A far more positive approach is to add plenty of moisture-retaining and rich humus-makers, such as compost, manure, etc., together with plenty of fertilizers.

Drainage. All plants need a soil that is moist, but well-drained. Very few plants can live with their roots perpetually submerged in stagnant water. Any soil that is waterlogged is also a soil from which air is excluded, and plants need air at the roots to live.

In soils in which these adverse conditions exist steps must be taken to improve the drainage. Usually good deep digging will achieve all that is necessary, but sometimes it is necessary to take more drastic steps and introduce drainage pipes. However, if the decision is taken to lay drainage pipes it is one that should be taken before undertaking the next task, so that the two can be done together.

Site Levelling. Site levelling is probably the most major task that will ever be undertaken in any garden. It must therefore be one of the first tasks to be undertaken, if it is to be undertaken at all. If you start with a sloping site you may well have to level it; certainly some level areas will improve the general appearance of the garden. If you start with a level site you may well want to introduce some changes to relieve the monotony of a single level garden.

The first operation in any site levelling or change of level job is to remove all the top-soil from the area to be levelled. The top-soil, which goes down for a spit (the depth of a spade), is the fertile soil in which plants grow. The sub-soil, which is the next spit down, is usually of a different colour and also much more tacky.

To determine the levels of a sloping site use thick bamboo canes of different lengths, a thick straight-edge about 6 ft. long and a spirit-level. Put a tent peg at the highest point of the garden and place a cane just under 6 ft. from it, making the top of the cane level with the peg with the help of the straight-edge and the spirit-level. The distance and height of the cane will then give you the angle of your slope. In this way the whole garden can be covered by a series of canes. To make different levels and slopes place other canes beside the marker canes you used to map the slopes. With these other canes you can work out absolutely horizontal lawns by using the spirit-level and straight-edge or devise new angles of slopes by making the other canes fall short or rise above the marker canes. T-shaped boning rods are used for sighting the angles of slopes by lining them up with eye over the top of the 'T'.

The best way to get a completely flat surface is by the 'cut and fill' method. Having first removed the top-soil, you then remove the sub-soil, transporting it from the higher levels to the lower levels, until the desired new level has been achieved. You then replace the top-soil, or import some, as the case may be, and level off with pegs and a spirit-level.

According to the way in which the pegs are worked out, this method may be used either to level an entire sloping site, or to convert the sloping site into a series of terraces. Similarly, higher areas can be created, as can sunken gardens. Where there are changes of level, measures will have to be taken to ensure that the levels remain constant, and do not slip away through weathering and natural subsidence. If the change in level is not great, a gentle slope covered either with grass (which may be difficult to mow) or with a shrub or mixed border can be used. Generally more satisfactory, however, is the use of retaining walls. These may be of either dry stone construction (which is useful in assisting drainage) or of bonded brick. In either case, the walls should be built on a firm foundation of concrete, and should be sloped back slightly against the level above them. An alternative is to use the change of level to create a rock-garden, but it is usually necessary to use fairly substantial blocks for this purpose.

Having created changes of level it is then obviously necessary to create a means of passing from one level to another: this will

EGION of
HONOR

▲ Some of the modern paeonies are among the finest of hardy perennial border plants. The longer they are left alone the better the flower.

Instant gardening is easy in these days of container-grown plants and garden centre supermarkets. All the plants shown here can be bought from any garden centre. If you don't like one year's scheme, dig it up and try something different. ▶

30

necessitate building a sloping path or a flight of steps. At this stage, it is worth bearing in mind that you will have to move such things as lawn-mowers and wheel-barrows from one level to another.

Borders and Lawns. Having levelled the site or created new levels in it, the next step is to mark out the borders, working strictly from your plan.

When marking out beds and borders it is useful to have a right-angled frame for getting the corners square. This is easily made by taking three pieces of straight-edged wood and screwing them together so that they form a triangle one side of which is a right angle. Curves and circles are marked with a fixed stake with a line attached to it, and another stake, the whole device being used in the same way as a pair of compasses.

To mark out an oval bed decide on the length and width. Using a radius of half the length make two curves or arcs from the two extreme points of the width. Where these two curves intersect insert a stake. There will be two points at which the curves intersect so insert a stake in each point. Then take a line which has a loop at each end and is exactly the same distance as the length of the proposed bed. Secure this line with the loops over the two stakes, and with a third stake score a line in the ground keeping the cord taut all the time. This will mark out a perfect oval of the prescribed length and breadth.

Having levelled the site and marked out the beds and borders, the next operation is the laying of the lawn. This operation is dealt with in detail in the chapter devoted to that subject.

Having created the lawn, then digging can begin. If the garden is large enough for a negative area, then digging can start here immediately.

Digging. The purpose of digging is to break up soil to admit air and to allow water free drainage through the soil particles. And soil that is well aerated and which drains freely is one in which a useful population can thrive.

If taken steadily, digging is one of the most rewarding of all gardening operations.

The type of digging in which you engage will depend on your analysis of the state of the soil. At this stage you will be most concerned about the problems of drainage and the soil structure and type, discussed above.

If the top-soil is thin, or the area has already been dug to the depth of two spits (two lengths of the blade of a spade) it will be necessary only to give the ground a plain digging. *Plain digging* means digging a trench one spit deep and turning over the next strip of soil into it, and so on. The soil from the first trench is taken to the end of the plot being dug and used to fill the trench made by the last strip of soil to be dug. Manure may be left on the surface of the dug ground in autumn to rot down into the soil.

It is generally agreed that rough digging of this kind is best done in the autumn or winter so that the action of frost can penetrate the uneven surface of the ground left by digging and so provide the crumb structure which the gardener is ultimately seeking. Digging at this time of year is particularly beneficial to clay soil.

Double digging enables you to improve the drainage of your soil because it reaches two spits or over 18 in. into the soil, which in many cases will be down to the sub-soil. This sub-soil is never lifted, but manure and compost and other fertilizers can be forked into it and it can be forked over to improve the drainage. You work across a wider stint, say 2 to 3 ft., and begin by taking out a trench one spit deep of this width at one end of the plot and wheeling the soil to the other. Or you can divide the plot into two narrow lengths and work down to the bottom and back, so that the earth you have taken out of your first strip is returned to the ground in space left by the removal of the last strip, which in this system will be adjoining the first one. When you have forked over and dug in compost or manure in the bottom of the first trench to the depth of a spit you dig a second trench behind the first, carefully turning over the sods so that the grass and weeds are placed upside down. Alternatively, you can slice off the top like a turf and lay it upside down in the trench and just dig the rest of the earth on to it. This method will enable you to examine the roots of the weeds like bindweed, dandelion, elder, nettles, couch grass and buttercup, which must always be removed from the soil altogether, as they are perennial and some will possibly grow again from the buried roots. Double digging is recommended for all new ground and is traditionally done at regular intervals on vegetable plots (3 years) and

▲   Lilies have a reputation for being difficult plants to grow. This is
quite untrue of the modern hybrids, like these Bellingham hybrids,
which you grow as you would any other border plant.

Another small garden in which a sense of distance has been created
in spite of the fence stopping the view at the far end of the garden. ▶

borders (4 years). If you use mechanical diggers instead you would probably set the tines to cut fairly deep and go over the whole area. Then spread the manure, etc., and go over the area with the digger again in the transverse direction to work in and break down the manure.

Double digging is sometimes known as half-trenching. Full *trenching* means digging a 3-ft. trench one spit deep and making one pile of the soil taken out at the other end of the plot. The trench is then divided into two and a second spit taken out of the first 18-in. strip. This soil, too, is removed to the other end of the plot, but kept in a separate pile from the first. The bottom of this 18-in. strip is then dug over to a spit and manure and compost forked into it. The other 18-in. strip of the 3-ft. wide trench is then dug to the depth of a second spit, the earth being turned over on to the first 18-in. strip. Like the first strip the third spit down of the second strip is then dug over and manured. A third 18-in. strip is then dug, the top spit going on to the first strip, and the second spit going on to the second strip, and proceeding in this way to the end of the plot where the two piles of soil wheeled there originally are returned, the top layer of soil going in last. The same measures for correcting drainage, mentioned above, may be taken during trenching, and it is also feasible to divide the plot into two as for double digging. Full trenching of this kind is obviously normally done only on top-soil at least two spits deep, and is carried out to increase the depth of fertile soil quickly. The process itself is rather laborious and it is best to tackle a part of the work each year.

Ridging is a form of digging similar to the previous ones, except that it results in exposing the soil to the frost's action more by increasing the amount of surface with ridges. It is very useful for heavy clays. As before, a trench a spit deep is dug and removed to the other end of the plot. The trench should be about 2 ft. wide. Starting at one end of the next, three spadefuls of soil, one behind the other, are turned over into the trench. The first will be furthest away, the second next to it, and the third on top to make the ridge. Or, it is sometimes preferable to lay the first spadeful in the centre and the other two at an angle to each other over it, also making a ridge. The plot is made into a line of ridges in this way.

Just as human beings need different foods for various purposes, so do plants. The three major plant foods, led by nitrogen which feeds the green parts of the plant, phosphorus for the roots and potassium for flowers and fruits, are known under the general heading of NPK, which are the distinguishing letters from their chemical formulae. Just as the humus-makers carry the food, the fertilizers are the food itself. Top-quality stable manure carries enough NPK for most plants in its natural state, and the other humus-makers also carry these foods in varying degrees. Generally, however it is necessary to supplement the humus-makers with fertilizers in order to increase the diet of chemicals that plants need. To speed plants properly give them plenty of animal manures and humus-makers, plus a general fertilizer containing nitrogen phosphates and potash, i.e. with a balanced NPK, and you can be assured of good crops, brilliant blooms and a general, healthy garden. Provided sufficient humus is worked into the soil, inorganic chemicals will not be

NPK Table		
Nitrogen		
Sulphate of ammonia (cheap)	Top dressing on growing plants	1 oz./sq. yd.
Nitrate of soda (cheap)	Top dressing quick acting	$\frac{1}{2}$–1 oz./sq. yd.
Hoof and horn (expensive)	Base dressing before sowing	4 oz./sq. yd.
Dried blood (expensive)	Base dressing at sowing or after	1–2 oz./sq. yd.
Phosphates		
Superphosphate (cheap)	Base dressing before sowing or planting	1–2 oz./sq. yd.
Basic slag (cheap)	Autumn or winter before sowing or planting	4 oz./sq. yd.
Bone meal (cheap)	Autumn or winter before sowing or planting	2–4 oz./sq. yd.
Potash		
Sulphate of potash (cheap)	Base dressing at sowing or planting	1–2 oz./sq. yd.
Wood ashes	Base dressing at any time	6–8 oz./sq. yd.

harmful if used sensibly. Organic fertilizers are of animal or vegetable origin; inorganics mostly come from minerals and are sometimes known as 'artificials'. Yet a third class are known as 'organic-based' which are artificially mixed organic and inorganic fertilizers.

'Golden Pride', one of the finest yellow roses of all, of a singularly pure yellow.

You can buy ready-mixed compounds of NPK in varying proportions or with other chemicals added to suit the needs of various types of plants. Balanced NPK in equal proportions for general use might be marked 7·7·7. An NPK compound fertilizer marked 10·5·5 would have 10 per cent nitrogen, 5 per cent phosphates and 5 per cent potash.

Other known chemicals required by plants include calcium, magnesium, boron, iron, manganese, copper, molybdenum, zinc, chlorine, cobalt, but only in minute amounts. These are known as 'trace' elements because only traces of them are needed in the soil.

Soil testing. One of the most important aspects of soil balance is the acid/alkali ratio. All garden soil is either acid or alkaline and the degree is measured on what is known as the pH scale from 0 to 14. Thus below 6·5 the soil is termed acid and above 7·5 it is alkaline. Some plants like ericas (below 5·5), hydran-

38

Clematis montana 'Rubens' is an ideal plant for hiding an unsightly shed.

geas, blue (below 5) and rhododendrons (below 4·5) thrive on acid soils, others like brassicas and lilac prefer more alkali in the soil. An acid soil is easily balanced by introducing lime. An alkaline soil with a very high pH is less easily corrected with additions of peat, compost and sulphate of ammonia. The amount of lime is not as good a measure as the pH, because some types of soil need more than others to correct acidity.

The simplest way to find out the state of your soil is get some test papers from a garden shop, mix up a little moist soil with some water in a saucer and leave for about 15 minutes. If your soil is acid give about ½ lb. of hydrated (concentrated) lime to sandy or loamy ground per sq. yd. On clay soil give ¾ lb. per sq. yd. More expensive kits will enable you to say more precisely, but the above is sufficient for most gardeners' needs.

Soil testing kits will help you to find out exactly how much NPK there is in your soil, or you can write to the county horticultural adviser c/o of your county council for his advice.

3 Larger Garden Design

As land gets scarcer, gardens get smaller. Anyone with a quarter of an acre or more has a large garden by today's standards. Most fortunate are those who have a *new* garden to create in an area of that size. Because undoubtedly, starting from scratch you can have a better, cleaner, more modern outlook from your home with the wide range of plants and materials now available.

If you are taking over an established plot, especially if it is fairly large, the chances are it will be cluttered with overgrown shrubs, darkened by high trees, laid-out and fashioned with old, cracked and weed-infested paving, an ill-placed rockery and a dirty pond. But whether you are starting from scratch or re-planning an existing garden, the same basic principles apply.

Much depends, of course, on your situation; the type of plot, its overall shape, where the house sits in relation to the main part of the garden. It is impossible to produce a blueprint that can be applied to every garden. In the end the choice of styling must always be your own.

Basically, in the design of larger gardens, we will be looking for: (1) A pleasant and interesting outlook for every window in the house, an outlook that blends with your home and is entirely compatible with it. (2) The creation of vistas, giving your garden a sense of distance, space and depth. (3) The inclusion of special features, such as rockeries, ponds, pergolas and terraces. (4) The element of surprise, discovered by visitors as

40

they walk round your garden. (5) An air of mystery, often created by dividing the garden into two or more sections, each in contrasting design.

Above all, your garden must suit your own special requirements and the amount of time you will be able to spend on it. It is important, therefore, to establish, truthfully in your own mind, the type of garden you really want.

The way your garden will look eventually is not the only important factor. Study how the land lies in relation to all points on the compass. Make a note of the general aspect, of shady or specially sunny areas, check for wind tunnels and particularly exposed places, look out for damp and waterlogged patches. All of these are vital when you are weighing up where to site your flower-beds, where to put screens and windbreaks, and where to build your 'sitting out' areas. With a larger garden, which may not be particularly well protected from the elements, these points are vital. So make a thorough survey and take notes on your findings.

Next, give some thought to the features which you might eventually like to include, a pool, a patio, arbour, terrace or rockery. Again, draw up a list so that you can sketch them in on your master-plan – even if you are unlikely to be able to start work on them for a season or two. One word of warning: don't try to include every possible style and feature in one garden; the result will be that each detracts from all the others. Confine yourself to two or three really good ideas, and work on them.

Planning. Having made some notes on the site, and having listed the main features desired, the time has come to start planning. Equip yourself with a thick pencil and several sheets of mathematical paper.

Rough out, to scale, accurate dimensions of your house and garden boundaries. Then get to work on the design itself. This is usually best done in three stages.

Stage one consists of a rough plan on which to map out paving and terracing around the perimeter of the house and also the general area of the lawns. Try to nominate a focal point, perhaps a large tree or shrub mid-way down the back garden. If there isn't a focal point, you will need to establish one. Designing a garden is like painting a three-dimensional picture and you will find it helpful to have some object on which to take your bearings, thus arriving at a design which has balance and which is in perspective.

On stage two of the plan, add the dominant features, such as trees and shrubs, walls, terraces, arches and so on, that will provide and establish the outline of the garden proper. The third stage is then taken up with mapping out your flower-beds, the paths that will take you round the garden, drawing in the special effects.

As the plan progresses remember to refer regularly to the notes on aspect so that all your garden's advantages and disadvantages can be fully taken into account.

The Design. Styling a garden can be compared with the way you furnish your home. It will reflect your own personal taste. The plants and features may be the same as your neighbours, but the way you combine them will be different.

The problem of creating an original garden is more difficult on entirely flat sites than it is on what initially appear to be difficult sites, those with dips and mounds and slopes.

For these natural contours can be used – and even exaggerated – to create sunken gardens, terraces, rockeries, miniature mountain streams, and so on. So if ever you had any thoughts of grading and levelling your rough plot – bear this in mind before setting to work to flatten it.

Level sites present something of a problem in creating interest. The special effects and vistas have to be created rather than adapted from natural resources and this requires good planning, and an appreciation of the use of colourful subjects.

An ultra-modern garden with clean-cut shapes, colourful patios and terracing will look completely out of place around an older type house. Similarly, a brand new house seems to call out for bright materials and a light and airy surrounding.

Whatever your choice, it is important that looking out from the house there is an immediate impression of space and light. Therefore the central area of the first part of your garden is best left open: trees and shrubs should be kept away from windows.

Flowering Crabs are among the most spectacular of trees for small gardens. They are beautiful in flower, fruit and autumn colour.

The exceptions of course, are climbing shrubs, like clematis and honeysuckle which can be trained close to the walls, and need not overshadow the windows.

It is also worth noting here that the roots of trees and hedges and even some of the more hefty shrubs, spread far and wide. They will very often throw up suckers which could ruin tarmac drives or patios and should be planted well away from your property. Willows send their roots in search of water and if the cement becomes weak, they could well find their way into the cracks in the drainage system, causing leakage and blockages.

On your plan, you will naturally start at the house and work outwards. It is often best to aim at a paved area around as much of the house as possible, and certainly at each entrance.

A fairly substantial patio will often prove a good idea; it may be built with steps up or down to the garden itself, according to your site. It is always more interesting if steps can be used instead of going straight on to the lawn.

There are many forms of paving available now. Slabs come in a wide range of sizes, colours, textures and finishes, and the design possibilities are limitless – the choice is yours.

Perhaps the easiest way of planning your patio and paved areas is to map out the design on a separate sheet of paper, using coloured pencils for the right effect. The patio may require edging, either with a low wall in block or stone or perhaps screen blocks for a higher type.

Again the choice is wide. But as with paving, it is important to be thoroughly satisfied with the design before getting on with the job.

For most people the lawn is the central feature of the garden – yet it is often the most neglected, ill-considered area. It needs the same close scrutiny as a flower-bed in selecting the variety of grass most suited for the wear and tear it will get. The commonly held view that lots of grass makes a garden easy to run is nonsense.

A lawn will need mowing once a week, sometimes twice, during the seven-month growing period; it will need treating for weeds, fertilizing, aerating, watering – and so on. If you establish a huge lawn entirely out of proportion with the size of your garden, you have nothing but a well-tended paddock.

The shape of the lawn will have a substantial effect on the

Garden 1. A very simple garden put down mainly to shrubs, lawn and paving. **A.** Semi-detached house with garage **B.** Sunken slabs **C.** Paved drive **D.** Pool **E.** Dustbins **F.** Fire **G.** Compost **H.** Table and bench **J.** Paved area with inset cobbles

1. Privet hedge **2.** Yucca **3.** Heather border **4.** Buddleia **5.** *Prunus amygdalus* 'Commalus' **6.** *Mahonia Aquifolium* hedge **7.** *Srobus discolor* **8.** *Paeonia lutea* 'Ludlowii' **9.** Ground cover of *Cotoneaster horizontalis*, Heathers, etc **10.** *Malus* 'Golden Hornet' **11.** *Hydrangea hortensis*

general view of your garden. A slim lawn will make the garden look longer, a shaped lawn will take the eye around with it and will give the impression of size.

Don't be afraid of unusual shapes. You might try a zig-zag effect for instance, repeated on a parallel basis each side of the lawn or, instead of running the grass area and general garden aspect from end to end, i.e. north to south or east to west, consider a diagonal approach laying the lawn across the garden, corner to corner.

Circular lawns also can be extremely effective and better still are double circles, one in the foreground of the garden, the second in the far part linked by paths and a covered archway.

Alternatively, to achieve a definite contrast between the first and second garden, use a circular shape in the foreground and a rectangular or octagonal shape in the second compartment.

As you move on to drawing in the second part of the garden, remember that some of it at least must be visible in the general view from the house and not entirely cut off – one section from the other.

Where it is possible to establish a series of gardens on different levels, the use of steps can be extremely effective. These help continue the line of the house into the garden and give the illusion of greater space.

Backgrounds. Having established the general format of the garden, now is the time to think of backgrounds.

The list of trees and shrubs, ornamental and flowering varieties, is endless, and it really is somewhat pointless recommending any specific type for an unspecified situation. But the general principle is to add height and depth to the perimeter of your garden without shutting off natural landscapes and this can be achieved even if it is necessary to install fencing or hedging, by careful and imaginative planting. It could be of a continuous line of one particular type of tree, with lower decks of bushy shrubs, banking down to the low-growing plants of the border.

Elsewhere in the garden – space permitting – you will want an assortment of trees and shrubs, but one has to be careful in siting trees. The charms of young weeping willows may turn into trouble in years to come as the tree reaches maturity.

Garden 2. A more complex garden for the somewhat keener gardener incorporating such features as a rock garden and a garden pond. **A.** Semi-detached house with garage **B.** Stone slabs **C.** Dustbins **D.** Garden shed **E.** Paving **F.** Pool **G.** Stone ornament of pedestal **H.** Bird bath **J.** Fire. **K.** Compost **L.** Barbecue with benches

1. Bedding out plants and spring bulbs **2.** Ground cover of *Gypsophila* 'Rosy Veil', *Stachys* 'Silver Carpet', vinca **3.** Rockery containing Polygonum, *Sedum purpureum*, Dianthus and Ferns **4.** Ground cover of Vero ica, *Genista lydia*, Thymus **5.** *Viburnum opulus* **6.** *Chamaecyparis fletcheri* **7.** *Acer japonicum* **8.** *Chamaecyparis fletcheri* **9.** *Deutzia* 'Mont Rose'

You may wish to plant trees or shrubs close together as wind-breaks, or as a screen for outbuildings, and in this case you will probably find that slim columnar conifers planted in groups of three or four are most suitable. One other word of caution: quick growing trees remain quick growing – and again could cause embarrassment as the trees mature.

The technique of repetition with tree planting is widely used. This means planting a columnar conifer, say, on each side of steps leading from one garden section to another. Or on opposite sides of the lawn.

Before you do any planting in the general run of the garden, take a look out from the windows of your house to ensure that vistas are not being spoiled and that unwanted shadows will not be cast – in future years – over the garden or house.

Permanent Features. The introduction of stone into any part of the garden scheme should serve a definite purpose, to raise or break levels, add a weather break, or make a wall leading to steps. Above all, it should fit in with the general character of the garden. Flag-stone paving, terraces with balustrades, flight of steps, dry stone walling, stone pillared pergolas are delightful features of gardens where they fit in with the environment.

But one must guard against losing beauty and aesthetic charm by the indiscreet use of stone. Try to give it an atmosphere of age. Stone can also be used effectively for raised beds. And there are numerous possibilities for low walls, alpine gardens and surrounds to pools.

Paths. The construction of 'service' paths – i.e. those that lead from house to outbuildings, the greenhouse and so on – should, of course, be carried out at an early stage of the new garden, probably at the time the house was built.

The paths which take you around your garden can be left until later, but naturally it is best to get as much of the messy construction work over with before the garden takes shape.

Paths can be effectively used to help in the creation of vistas. They can lead in curves or straight lines to your inner gardens and special features. They can turn unexpectedly to behold a rockery screened from the general view.

Garden 3. A design incorporating a vegetable area. **A.** Semi-detached house with garage **B.** Gravel drive **C.** Paving **D.** Dustbins **E.** Sand pit **F.** Swing **G.** Garden seat **H.** Bird bath on raised paving **J.** Green house **K.** Compost **L.** Fire

1. Spirea Arguta **2.** Ground cover plants, e.g. Genista, *Iberis* 'Snowflake', heathers **3.** Rose border **4.** Trellis with climbing roses **5.** Rockery containing *Genista lydia*, Androsace, Erikas **6.** Herb garden **7.** Vegetable garden **8.** Gooseberries, blackcurrants and raspberries **9.** Salad garden **10.** Apple trees **11.** Pear trees **12.** Runner beans **13.** *Prunus sargentii*

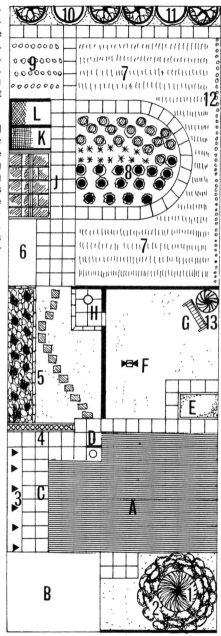

49

A striking small garden. The garden has been created as a picture to look at, yet retains a sense of mystery.

There should be as few main paths as possible; try to avoid them giving your garden a formal look.

Borders and Beds. The extent of your borders and beds will depend on personal choice. Certainly, there will be the space to accommodate all requirements and one should remember, when selecting and designing your floral displays that formalized beds can act as a striking contrast to the ragged look if you have the facility for a divided garden.

Rose gardens should in general be designed on a formal or geometrical plan, such as a circle or rectangle, and there are numerous other plants which lend themselves to this sort of treatment.

Another unusual element in the design of beds and borders can be achieved by massing flowering plants of a single colour together so that you have whites, blues, reds, oranges and so on –

n attractive terrace to an older-style house. ne magnolia on the wall is nearly 70 years d. *Courtesy of the Cement and Concrete* *ssociation.*

Day lilies look lovely beside a path. You can buy them in reds, pinks, yellows and oranges.

all in separate beds.

To help cut the amount of work involved, a number of shrubs can be included in flower borders. They can also be used to create a sense of depth in borders by building up a bank of flowers, from tiny dot plants to tallish shrubs, interspersed with lupins, hollyhocks and delphiniums.

Try to choose summer flowering shrubs to blend with the flowering times of your herbaceous plants lower down.

As with trees, the repetition of particularly outstanding plants in a herbaceous border helps with the overall design effect.

Replanning an Old Garden. Creating a new garden from an old one can be more of a headache than starting from scratch.

Before you even contemplate a mass razing operation, take a good look around and try to discover the garden that existed before and the reasons your predecessor had for his various planting schemes. Clear the ground of weeds, taking care not to injure too many plants in the process; walk round and cover it inch by inch and see if you can establish the original plan.

The order of priorities in which you tackle the neglected garden is entirely different from that of a new garden. Never begin by embarking on any major constructional work, such as re-shaping rockeries, re-establishing a water garden or building a patio.

The first task is to bring the growing sections back to life. This may well take a whole season and, while you are engaged on this reclamation, the overall plan you wish to adhere to will begin to take shape. The trees and shrubs you decide to keep can be pruned back into shape so that you can get an idea of your backgrounds and colour schemes. Beware of overpruning, however, in the first year. Too drastic cutting may be more than these already neglected plants can stand and they will die.

If you have to take any trees out, never cut them off at the stump. With manageable trees, lop off the high branches and those that are in your way; then dig around the roots and sever the main roots with an axe. This will enable you to rock the tree backwards and forwards, and with more root cutting you will eventually be able to push it over.

Front Gardens. With a quarter of an acre plot or more, it is likely that you will have a fair amount of space to play with at the front of the house. This is not an invitation to elaborate schemes. Front gardens – unless they are on specially awkward sites – should be simple; just enough shielding with trees and shrubs to afford a degree of privacy from passers-by.

A fairly open outlook from the windows is called for. Properties of all ages can be set off admirably with a 'clothing' of climbers for the front wall. You will have a double viewing situation to cater for – one from the house, the other from the road.

The lawn area can be used to shape the garden and it is probable that your drive and paths will have some bearing on this factor also.

The use of trees and shrubs can also be effective in establishing the shape, and remember the repetition ingredient which is

Garden 4. A more complex garden for the somewhat keener gardener incorporating features such as a rock garden and a garden pond. **A.** Semi-detached house with garage **B.** Paving slabs **C.** Cavity wall with pendulous rock plants **D.** Dustbins **E.** Compost **F.** Fire

1. Heathers **2.** Rock garden containing *Saxifraga anchusa*, gypsophila, gentians, etc. **3.** Small pool containing dwarf water lilies, etc. **4.** *Kolkwitzia amabalis* **5.** Rose bed **6.** Climbing roses **7.** Trellis with *Clematis* 'Montana Rubens' **8.** Child's garden **9.** Flowering cherry (*Prunus* 'Ukon') **10.** Salad garden **11.** Herb garden **12.** Ground cover plants, e.g. *Cotoneaster horizontalis*, Thymus, Gypsophila **13.** Flowering Almond (*Prunus amygdalus*) **14.** Lilac ('Fermament') **15.** Buddleia **16.** Two forsythias **17.** Laburnum Tree, spring bulbs encircling trees

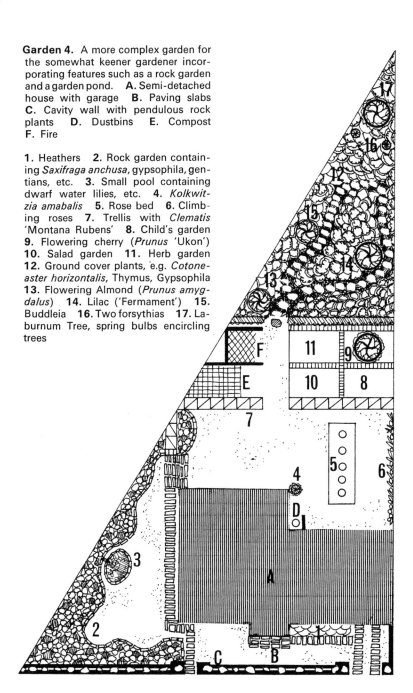

Conifers are very fashionable at the moment. Many of the dwarf forms and varieties are ideal plants for small gardens, needing little attention. They do not get on well with dogs!

No garden is too small to make colourful. Hydrangeas, cotoneaster and wisteria give colour through the year.

particularly useful at the front with, for example, columnar conifers on either side of the drive.

On the boundaries, try to avoid hedging. For gardens of this size they tend to emphasize the enclosed look. Some sort of barrier, such as ranch-fencing, wicket fence, or heavy chains between posts, looks far more effective, supported by some imaginative plantings of trees and shrubs.

A trouble-free front garden. The pond makes a feature in the midst of the paving and bedding plants supply colour in summer, bulbs in the spring.

4 Small Garden Design

By comparison with the lavish way in which one can approach the planning and design of larger gardens, the smaller plots that are so much more familiar these days present special limitations – and a special challenge.

The house itself will necessarily influence the style of the garden, both back and front. Boundaries are more visible and confining and need special attention. They will also affect the design, particularly in the attempt to create vistas.

The smaller the garden, the more important it is to answer two vital questions: What do you want from your garden? How much work do you want to put in? Design is also affected these days by the enforced factors in the development of large housing estates. Many developers have what can only be described as a mania for complete uniformity with open plan fronts and squared off backs – often with the same sort of fencing. It is therefore necessary to look closely at the problem of 'clothing' or hiding these boundary fixtures.

You may also be faced with hiding a neighbour's cabbage patch or washing line clearly visible through a chain-link fence. And, of course, you will want to achieve some degree of privacy from overlooking property.

At the same time, if the garden next door is an established one you will do well to take account of those of your neighbour's plants and trees that are visible from your garden – and use them in drawing up your own planting schedule.

These will all need your attention in weighing up where you are siting taller trees and shrubs which affect the outline of your design. One word of caution. Forest trees are generally not advisable in these confined areas. There are many subjects more suited to smaller gardens.

An evergreen shield of *Cupressocyparis leylandii* is an ideal subject for a background. It can be cropped and topped at the desired height. Where wind is not a problem, *Chamaecyparis lawsoniana* will make a good 8-ft. screen and is easier to control for height.

Once you have established your needs, the planning can begin. As with the creation of larger gardens it is necessary to draw up a plan of the design.

Again there is no single answer or master plan that can be applied to what will be a thousand and one different situations. The basic principles, however, remain the same.

The outlook to the garden is likely to be confined to the front and back, with little or no side garden. It may be a long slim plot or a short, fat one. So the task of creating a sense of space and distance, and of establishing pockets of interest which are not immediately visible at first glance, becomes more difficult.

Before starting planning the garden you need to look closely at the site, weigh up the aspect – i.e. assessing to which points of the compass the garden is exposed.

Open aspects, for instance, will require screening and breaks from the biting winds, from north and east. It is also important to take into account which points of the garden will be put into shade by buildings or trees. This is not to say that you should avoid causing shaded areas – these can themselves help add depth and beauty. But you should exploit those situations that you find in your garden.

Sites which are exposed to a westerly aspect are favourable to plants which are only just in the 'hardy' classification. Southern aspects are to be used to the fullest extent with an abundance of plants which crave for the sun. Southerly aspects are suitable for all the most popular plants, like roses, dahlias, sweet peas, vegetables and so on.

Sites facing the north are more likely to be prone to lingering frost pockets and generally lower temperatures.

Easterly aspects will get biting winds. So bear all these points in mind as you draw up your plan.

Note, too, other problems such as poor drainage, wind tunnels and so on, so that remedial action or precautionary measures can be taken as the garden takes shape.

Looking from the house out, a focal point is necessary as you prepare to paint the garden picture.

At a suitable point about three-quarters of the way down the garden, perhaps at a curve in the lawn, try to establish a fixture that draws the eye, a specimen shrub, for instance, like a magnolia, a maple, or a group of medium-high conifers. Or perhaps a pergola over a secondary 'sitting out' area; or an arbour or portico. It is around some feature as this that the rest of the garden can be created.

The aim even with smaller plots is to give the impression of space. In general one should try to round the corners of the boundaries, softening the harsh, fenced-in corners with flowering shrubs, or with a screen or pergola hiding a vegetable patch. At the other extreme do not fall into the trap of cutting out too many island beds in the lawn. They merely tend to destroy any sense of space that might be created by the lawn. One or two bold island beds are all that a small garden can take.

So what is the design solution to the formal rectangular plot, of say 100 ft. by 40 ft., which is about the average size of new gardens today?

After establishing your focal point the major item to consider is the lawn. It creates what garden designers call the open centre – a usually level area of quiet around which the garden can flow. The greenness of the grass acts as a foil to the colourfulness of flowers.

Avoid at all costs square or rectangular lawns. Try to create instead a lawn with pleasant curves, perhaps accentuated at a convenient point by a row of small, slow-growing conifers, or a selection of low-growing shrubs that will tend to hide part of the garden from a first-glance.

The curved lawn will lead the eye away and save some of the features for a second look.

The front part of the lawn should be kept open, to give the impression of space. The curve is perhaps best brought in at about the middle of the lawn with a mixed border and shrubs

Hostas, especially the variegated ones, have big, bold leaves and make excellent plants for a shaded part of the garden. The one shown here is *Hosta decorata*.

No garden is too small for a pond. The one shown here is in fact situated on a roof garden.

cutting well into it – but not hiding entirely the remaining part of your garden. It may even be possible to create a second garden, part of which should be visible from the first. But, of course, this becomes more difficult in smaller plots.

If you follow this plan you will have, from the house looking out, first an open space, then an eye-catching feature midway down the garden, with perhaps a path curving round one side of the lawn, part of it going beneath a pergola.

You will need to draw in on your plan at a fairly early stage – usually after deciding the shape of your lawn – the permanent features such as a rock-garden, a pool or pergola.

You can then lead your paths to and past these features and try to make part of them hidden from the general view from the house so that the element of surprise is introduced.

Consider also using these fixtures to hide inescapable garden eyesores – such as compost heaps, which are bound to be more clearly visible in the smaller garden. Trellis can be used effectively to hide eyesores and to divide small gardens, but do try to use it to train plants that give some sort of year-round foliage. A huge trellis full of sweet peas looks marvellous in summer. And a bank of runner beans even has its merits for looks and as a shield. But both would look awfully bare in winter.

Imaginative planting of individual or small groups of conifers and shrubs will also help to hide part of your garden from first glance. The division of the garden into two or more sections, or terraces, is the aim in most designs. But, of course, this is not always practicable in smaller gardens.

The pitfall to avoid in trying to make your garden look larger than it really is, is not to overdo the creation of these vistas or overcrowd your garden with tall and bushy subjects and special features. Simplicity is often the rule with confined spaces. Don't try to have more than one or two features. If you do you will end up with a cluttered mess which will be the complete reverse of your intentions.

A curve cut into the lawn, for instance, may not be entirely feasible with a short fat plot. So try and get away from the formal look imposed by the boundaries by making the lawn circular or oblong, with perhaps an island bed in the centre.

Colour Content. Let us now progress to the borders and beds. Again, it is impossible to suggest anything other than in general terms. But in planning, try to aim at a mixture of subjects that will give you year-round colour – not necessarily in flowers, but with foliage and berries too.

This is important because the careful and imaginative selection of brilliantly hued plants and colourful blooms can do much to enhance the look and, in the end, style and dimensions of the garden.

The greys of lavender, rosemary and senecio, for instance, can contrast beautifully with the red berries and apple green leaves

Garden 5. A more complex garden for the somewhat keener gardener incorporating features such as a rock garden and a garden pond. **A.** Detached house with garage **B.** Gravel drive **C.** Crazy paving **D.** Sun dial **E.** Compost **F.** Fire **G.** Trellis covering garden seat **H.** Swing **J.** Concrete, table and seat **K.** Sand pit **L.** Dustbin

1. Rock garden containing *Campanula portenschlagiana*, Arabis, *Primula auricula* **2.** Pool **3.** Five *Cupressocyparis leylandii* **4.** *Pyrus salcifolis* **5.** Ground cover of *Spirea alpina*, Helianthemum, Thymus, etc **6.** Holly hedge **7.** Apple tree **8.** Pear tree **9.** *Clematis lasurstern* **10.** Rose beds **11.** Children's garden **12** *Robina frisia*

of the taller shrub *Skimmia foremanii* or *Pernettya mucronata* with a choice of white, pink, lilac and crimson berries.

Again, attention to these contrasts can help in creating depth on the perimeter in what could well in fact be a fairly narrow bed in front of a fence.

The underplanting of bulbs and bays of dwarf plants at the foot of evergreens and individual shrubs is a good way of establishing an herbaceous border. Although the shrubs can thrust forward to the edge of the border at regular intervals, it would be useless to plant dwarfs further back than the middle of the border.

The planting of groups of dwarfs partly hidden by taller plants is another way of creating surprises in small gardens.

Where the planting area near fences is particularly small, use the fences themselves to help provide the backcloth to your design schemes. There are many climbing plants that can be used for this purpose.

Clematis is an excellent choice – and there are sufficient varieties to provide a long-flowering season. Vigorous, fence-hugging climbing roses of 6 ft. high or more are also excellent.

Fences like this are also most suitable to accommodate fruit-growing on a small scale – with horizontal or fan-trained trees, pears, plums or peaches.

Sunken Gardens. If you are faced with an entirely flat garden, it could well be helped by creating a change in the levels – and one of the most effective ways is a sunken garden.

The base of the sunken garden is most likely to be in crazy paving, reached by a single set of steps from the main level of the garden. The wall could be in the form of a rockery, and it should slope outward from the top.

Use the top-soil from your excavations to fill in around the stones, for planting up. Plant the surrounding area in the same way that you would a rockery or heather garden. The effect can be magnificent.

Heather in Design. The use of heathers as a labour-saving feature is dealt with in detail in a later chapter, but let us look briefly at the varied uses of heather in designing your garden.

Some gardens are prone to acid pockets in the soil and this

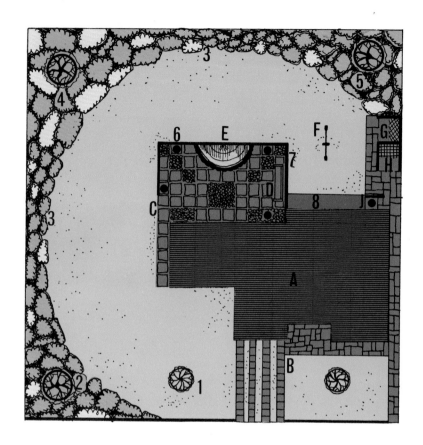

Garden 6. A very simple garden put down mainly to shrubs, lawn and paving.
A. Detached house with garage **B.** Paved drive **C.** Paving and cobbles
inside wall **D.** Stone bench **E.** Raised pool **F.** See-saw **G.** Fire
H. Compost **J.** Dustbins

1. Cupressocyparis **2.** Sorbus hybrid Gibbsii **3.** Ground cover of Helianthemum, Polygonum, Umbrosa, etc **4.** *Malus* 'Lemoinei' **5.** *Prunus* 'Kanzan'
6. Agapanthus in urns **7.** Wall planted with petunias and spring bulbs
8. Herb garden

will certainly affect the way you plan. Heathers can be used to beat this problem, since they will flourish in this type of soil.

In fact, a heath garden can be made on lime or acid soil where nothing else will grow. They are also effective for steep banks or undulating slopes and it is in these situations that they look and grow more naturally.

The shape of the heath garden should be as informal as possible and planting done in bold, irregular groups with the smaller varieties on the edge. Once established they give little trouble.

Shaded Areas. Do not try to eliminate shade altogether. Shade has an important part to play, particularly in the summer when heat may need tempering.

Many of our flowering shrubs and plants prefer shade rather than the full sun. And they will need shade at the hottest time of year to prevent scorching of foliage and flowers.

In your planning, therefore, consider well the habit, form and height of the various subjects you wish to plant, graduating them evenly from front to back, placing in the open those which like the sun and underplanting in shaded areas those that thrive better in these cooler, moist situations.

The use of shade itself can be taken into account when you are weighing up the possibilities for adding depth to your garden. And of course it can also be used admirably for your sitting-out areas.

Children in the Garden. A family with young children will want, initially, a garden to play in rather than to look at, so the design can be a progressive one to allow for additions, re-styling and planting when the children get older.

They will want at first a good paved area at the back of the house to play on when the lawn is wet.

They will want a fair-sized lawn to set up their wickets and goal posts. So the outlook and view from the house will naturally be an open one, probably throughout the garden.

But the creation of vistas can still be obtained in this garden, as can attractive beds, special features like the rockery, raised flower-beds and a good range of trees and shrubs. Pools of any sort where youug children are to play are generally rather risky.

Beds of tender plants will need to be kept well away from the lawn, and the trees and shrubs you choose should be fairly sturdy.

The beds can still be carved out to give your lawn an attractive shape. It is best to use heathers or low sturdy shrubs as a ground cover for close planting to the lawn. You can even walk on heathers without doing much damage. Later, when the children appreciate the garden more, the heathers can be moved and replaced with more colourful subjects if required.

Paving and Patios. Formal or informal, paving is an aspect of garden making that can make or mar the finished result. Of all forms of paving, precast concrete slabs are by far the most convenient and offer the greatest scope for imaginative design. The range of slabs available is tremendous – different sizes, colours, textures and finishes – and the design possibilities are increased almost limitlessly by the possibility of combining standard precast slabs with other types of paving.

Patterned walks, patios and other paved areas can be designed to suit the particular situation or the gardener's individual taste.

Perhaps the easiest way of going about the job is to buy a large pad of square-ruled graph paper and a box of coloured pencils. Using measurements taken on the site, the area to be paved can be drawn out roughly to scale and a whole range of possible patterns sketched out and considered before ordering the paving slabs.

It is particularly important when planning one's own paving pattern to be thoroughly satisfied with the design before getting on with the job. Generally, it is better to underplay contrasts in colour or texture rather than overdo them. Use one or two closely matching colours or textures for most of the work, with contrasting areas used sparingly for accent. This will usually be more satisfying in the long term.

Laying paving is not difficult. The ground should be dug out to the required level and well compacted. If the ground is on the soft side, roll in a layer of hardcore thoroughly and finish off with a level layer of fine granular material.

Set out string lines to keep the edges of the slabs in line and then start at one end bedding the slabs. Leave between $\frac{3}{8}$ in. and

A view from the terrace. The azaleas make a blaze of brilliant colour in early summer.

The point of a patio is to provide a trouble-free area in which to sit and enjoy the sun and the garden. *Courtesy Edwin H. Bradley & Sons Ltd.*

$\frac{1}{2}$ in. space between the slabs and bed each slab on five small piles of mortar about 2 in. high: one near each corner of the slab and one in the centre.

Tap each slab down to the required level with a wooden mallet until there is no tendency to rock: by using small pats of mortar rather than an over-all mortar bed the levelling will be easier and in the event that adjacent slabs settle unevenly the offending slab or slabs can be lifted off with a spade and re-levelled.

Joints can be filled with mortar which should be rubbed to a slight hollow with the thumb or a short length of dowel or round steel bar. As an alternative, slabs may be spaced more widely – say 2 in. – and the gaps filled with strips of turf or seeded with a close-growing plant: camomile is attractive and hardy, and the fragrance as it is stepped on is a pleasant bonus.

Crazy paving is also widely available in a range of colours and textures. Broken plain paving can also often be obtained from local councils. It is best laid by bedding on pats of mortar. The informal appearance is enhanced if joints between individual slabs are allowed to vary somewhat in width, and if the edges of the path or paved area are left ragged. Too-precise

Garden 7. A design incorporating a vegetable area. **A.** Semi-detached house with garage **B.** Paving **C.** Bird bath **D.** Patio **E.** Dustbins **F.** Sunken stone slabs **G.** Garden shed **H.** Compost **J.** Fire

1. Yuccas **2.** Cherry tree **3.** Apple tree **4.** Pear tree **5.** Plum tree **6.** Cooking apple tree **7.** Flower border of shade plants ground cover and lilies **8.** Copper beech **9.** Trellis with sweet peas **10.** Two *Paeonia lutea* 'Ludlowii' **11.** *Acanthus mollis* **12.** Runner beans at back of trellis **13.** Vegetable garden. **14.** Cordon gooseberries **15.** Herb garden **16.** Currant bushes **17.** Salad garden

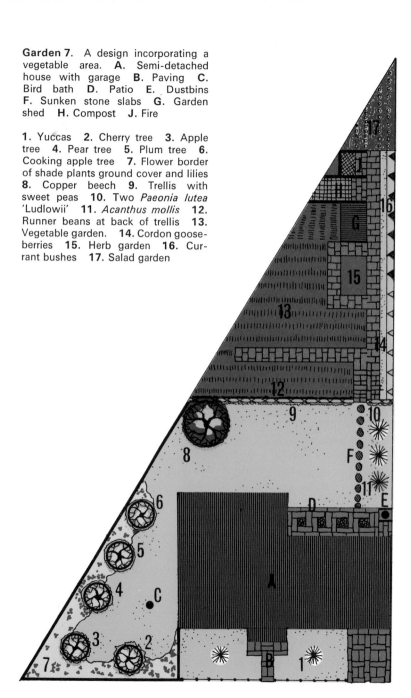

joints and edges destroy the casual effect, and result in something that looks rather like a carefully-assembled jigsaw puzzle.

Another cheap, and quite attractive, path or patio can be obtained from old coloured bricks. These can be readily available from a local demolition yard. They can be laid to any pattern and are quite durable. They should be laid on about three inches of hardcore for solidity. Beware of one danger, however; they tend to become slippery during wet weather.

The sheer permanency of concrete rules it out as far as many people are concerned. But for various reasons it may have to be your choice of material for patios or paths, so let us look at its advantages as a design feature.

If nothing else, concrete is certainly durable. It will last almost indefinitely; it is resistant to weather, and provided the job is done well in the first place it should never need repairing or replacing. Another advantage is its versatility, and nowadays the range of colours and finishes available is quite extensive.

What is vital when using concrete is that you are absolutely accurate in measuring out the proportion of sand to cement. You must also be sure of obtaining the right type of sand for the job you intend to do. So please, take advice from an expert before you start. While good concrete is durable, bad concrete will fail quickly and develop into a horrible, cracked and craggy eyesore.

For large areas, such as a patio, your best bet will probably be to buy the cement ready mixed. Firms who supply it operate in most parts of the country. Alternatively, for a big job to be done in small stages, you can buy the ready-mixed materials in dry form in quite small quantities.

Steps, Pergolas and Walk-ways. Steps in the garden can be used to continue the lines of the house and the patio into the garden itself.

A variety of materials can be used. Flat stone, slabs, concrete – even rustic logs – or just plain grass. Each material will need different treatment for laying – but all will need a food foundation of at least 6 in. of hardcore.

There is a place in most gardens for a pergola or walk-through archway. At front or back doors, or over the patio – a pergola can look beautiful with a tub-grown clematis, or

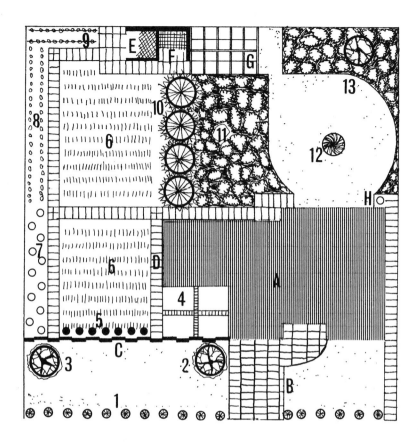

Garden 8. A design incorporating a vegetable area. **A.** Detached house with garage **B.** Paving **C.** Ornamental wall **D.** Paved walks **E.** Fire **F.** Compost **G.** Greenhouse **H.** Dustbins

1. *Chamaecyparis lawsoniana* 'Green Hedger' **2.** Crab Apple tree **3.** Plum tree **4.** Herb garden **5.** Blackcurrant bushes **6.** Vegetable garden **7.** Gooseberry bushes **8.** Strawberries **9.** Runner beans **10.** Chamaecyparis conifers **11.** Ground cover of Aster Dwarf Hybrids, Veronica, Saxifraga **12.** *Forsythia spectabilis* **13.** *Robinia frisia*

A corner of a garden turned into an attractive feature with a white-washed wall, an oil jar and a wrought iron gate.

honeysuckle, or perhaps a climbing rose or two depending on the size you can accommodate.

In smaller gardens, the construction can be quite simple. The easiest form is one made entirely of timber, using oak or the cheaper chestnut or larch. The uprights should be set two feet deep in concrete and can take the form of a lean-to at the side of the house, or as a walk-way.

If you want to be more ambitious, try a stone or brick piered construction; the piers can be two or three feet in height, with room for soil around the top for planting. Or the piers can go right up to the cross-members. The cross-members should protrude at least one foot over the uprights or piers, and remember to treat all woodwork in preservatives.

Walls, Fences and Hedges. Your choice of boundary barriers should be well considered – for a bad choice will undoubtedly ruin your whole design. Fences and high walls tend to foster claustrophobia, but are often unavoidable, particularly when an instant barrier is required.

Ranch-fencing can look attractive in the right setting and there are some new kinds of concrete fencing. It is really important to decide what your garden really needs to set it off. The effect of stone can fail totally if there is too much of it. For patios and high shields close to the house, screen blocks can be used to good effect, particularly when they are used with various kinds of factory-made walling stone.

If you are a do-it-yourself gardener, there are a number of points to bear in mind for a satisfactory job. It is no more difficult than building a brick wall, but remember you will need rather more mortar at the joints and regular piers for support.

For concrete blockwork, ordinary cement and sand are too strong. Using a slightly weaker mixture of masonry cement and builders' sand – not concreting sand – in a one to five proportion will ensure that any cracks that develop through settlement or temperature changes will follow the line of the mortar and will not crack the blocks. Then you can repoint if necessary. Mortar joints should be about $\frac{3}{8}$ in. thick and the blocks should be laid to a bond, with staggered vertical joints as with brickwork.

Another reason in favour of screen blocks is that they can eliminate one of the major problems caused by high barriers – that of creating airless areas in the garden that are conducive to pests and disease.

It is vital that a garden is able to breathe. Air movement is essential to all plants and assists in the moisture movement from the leaves. The moisture is taken up by the roots. If this movement does not exist, the whole atmosphere can be damp. Lawns may take hours to dry out after a heavy dew; frost pockets may occur; disease can become prevalent. These are some of the dangers of absolute seclusion. So in siting your

Garden 9. A very simple garden put down mainly to shrubs, lawn and paving. **A.** Semi-detached house with garage **B.** Paved area **C.** Table and bench **D.** Dustbins **E.** Patio **F.** Sand pit **G.** Climbing frame roofed with polygonum **H.** Sun dial **J.** Fire **K.** Compost

1. Tubs containing geraniums **2.** *Magnolia stellata* **3.** Fantrained pear **4.** *Symphoricarpus*, 'Mother of Pearl' **5.** Round bed containing three *Yuccas filamentosa* with ground cover of heathers **6.** Tub containing rhododendrons **7.** Four chamaecyparis conifers **8.** Two *Cotoneaster franchettii* **9.** Vinca

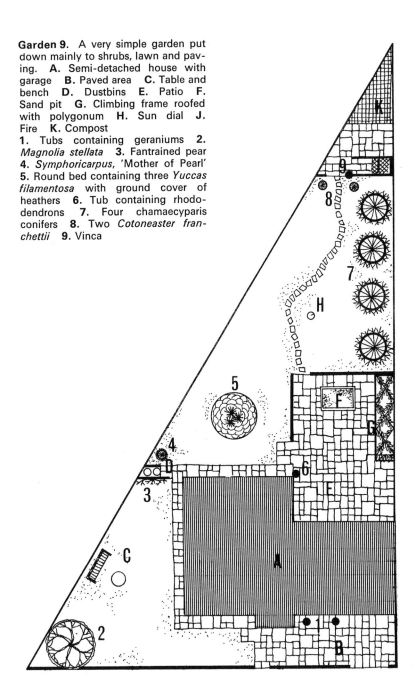

boundary barriers, try to make sure that this air movement is not unduly affected.

If you decide upon a hedge rather than a fence or wall, give considerable thought to the type you want. Allow air movement at the base. Another tip with hedges: if it is at all possible, run your paths alongside them. There are two reasons for this. First, when you are clipping the hedge, it will be easier to collect the debris; secondly, most forms of hedging require a good root run and this can be detrimental to other subjects in the near-by border. A hedge will not only affect the colour and design contrasts in your garden, but can also govern how much time you will have to spend maintaining your garden in the future. A quick growing hedge, for instance, remains quick growing and at the peak time of the year will need cutting more often than hedges of less vigorous growth.

Front Gardens. Small front gardens present their own special challenge. Because of the smallness of the area, tall trees are usually out of the question since they will cut off the light from the front window. You will be better off with a couple of slim trees backed up with bushes or low-growing shrubs, just to give a shade of privacy from passers-by.

One solution is to turn your whole front garden over to a special feature – like terraced paving with containerized plants – with one or two slabs left out for planting with heathers or dwarf conifers. Alternatively you could try a sunken garden or an alpine garden. Always avoid a square patch of lawn and a few dot plants in the border.

If the 'open plan' is your lot, try to bend the rules by planting tiny, young conifers that will take some years to grow; plant roses that can become bushier and more vigorous as the years pass (by which time those responsible for that open plan covenant may no longer be interested). Another way of breaking the monotony is to plant a border of heathers, or a herb hedge which will be initially low, but could discreetly climb to 4 ft. in a few years.

Finally, 'clothed' walls of climbers and container-grown plants that can be moved to strategic positions out front will all help overcome this garden system imposed upon us by the planners of our towns and cities.

▲ A new house in a new garden. This shows how quickly an attractive garden can be made after the builders move out. This picture was taken less than a year after the bungalow was completed. More ambitious schemes can follow later.

Bedding schemes need careful planning. Here brilliant red begonias are contrasted with silver-leaved plants and with plants with yellow mottled foliage. ▶

5 Unusually Sited Gardens

From the point of view of the amount of sheer hard labour that goes into the creating of a garden, those with gardens on more or less level sites are at a distinct advantage over those with awkward sites. On the other hand, the design possibilities of many awkward sites are far more interesting than those of flat sites. However, the basic design principles for awkwardly sited gardens are the same as those for level gardens.

Terracing comes to mind immediately we talk of gardening on slopes, and in many cases this may be entirely necessary. Indeed, if your plot provides the scope for such a development, all well and good.

There is seldom any problem with terracing a site on a slope falling from the house. The main point to bear in mind is that part of each terrace going down should be visible from the top. Where possible, elements of surprise should be incorporated along the paths down.

There are some sites, however, which do not lend themselves to this sort of approach. This is never more true than when a slope rises rather steeply immediately from the house.

A short, wide plot that may have a boundary fence at the top of the slope, or a shield of trees, is not the one for terracing. A different, less formal, approach is one that ought to be applied here, perhaps with a selection of small gardens within the whole garden, i.e. for heathers, rockeries, even a falling stream, all reached by a winding path accentuated by specimen trees and shrubs.

Terracing on gently rising slopes is quite permissible since one can achieve a sort of rolling, undulating impression with banks, rather than strict walled-in sections. But in this case, try to hide the linking features, such as paths and steps, since these tend to emphasize the fall to the house and thus shorten the vista.

Terraces need not be symmetrical, and can easily be curved or slanted. Indeed curving may be necessary if you are to follow the natural contours of the site. A long, gently-rising upward slope is better for the creation of vistas, but a downward slope offers more scope for the surprise elements.

Terraced sites, particularly those on hillsides, can present severe exposure problems and it is necessary to know how your site will be affected by biting winds, frosts and rain. You can then choose your plants accordingly and build in some shield features where desirable. If your slope is in the back garden, the front part of the terracing will be in the form of a patio with steps out to the garden proper. Alternatively, the terracing may go traversely and not be immediately connected to the house, in which case linking paths will be necessary from the flat around the house to the rising or falling grade. On larger plots, consider emphasizing these entrances to the terracing with covered walk ways or conifer-lined paths, etc.

A lawn on gently rolling sites can be extremely attractive – even on steeper banks, so long as you have the right sort of mower. But on slopes it is vital to get it free of hollows or bumps – otherwise you will get scalping. They should be eliminated by lifting the turf up and scraping or adding earth accordingly.

Hillside Gardens. Hillside gardens may seem an almost impossible hurdle to establishing a normal garden. But unless they are bounded by tall trees on all sides, such gardens will invariably get sunshine for part of the day, and if they face anywhere within the southern arc of the sun they will catch more than their fair share.

In order to accommodate plants, however, it will be almost essential to terrace the site, so that the growing areas can be made a less acute angle than 30 degrees, for if steeper it will be

Modern garden furniture is a far cry from traditional rustic discomfort. The paving here is a striking example of just what can be achieved with simple materials.

difficult to stop soil erosion and enable efficient cultivation of the ground, especially if vegetables, fruit and bedding plants are grown.

The use of winding paths towards the top, interconnected with broad, terraced cross-walks, is perhaps best. They will give many levels to the garden, from which attractive views can be had up and down.

If the house is old then soft brick or stone looks better for terrace walls than bright reconstructed stone or concrete blocks. One of the best types of stone for terraces is random-squared in which the blocks are of different sizes. But this is the most expensive. Poured concrete is cheaper, but it is very permanent and not very attractive.

▲ An attractive modern town garden designed by an architect. Such architectural gardens need little maintenance. *Courtesy of the Cement and Concrete Association.*

Another architect-designed garden. Here much more use has been ▲ made of flowering shrubs to soften the harshness of modern building materials. *Courtesy of the Cement and Concrete Association.*

Part of the fun of making a hillside garden is the gradual fitting of the constructional features to the landscape, so they must be flexible enough to accommodate changes as you progress. Moreover, apart from having a rough plan, it is almost impossible, without skilled advice, to visualize what the best layout will be, of both plants and materials, when you start.

Any excavation to provide level areas will provide valuable soil for beds. For paths, avoid gravel and bricks for the slopes as they are much too slippery, especially in winter. Asphalt gives a good grip, and so does ribbed concrete, or rough stone.

The real answer for connecting a hillside garden, however, is steps, and very beautiful layouts can be made, with curving steps, flanked by low retaining walls, topped by cavities for plants, and perhaps in other places the use of dry walls, filled with plants, can also be a special feature.

Rock-gardens can also be built in the intermediate spaces between waterfall levels too, and on the various levels of terracing wide bays can be created here and there so breaking the general line.

If you like pergolas for climbing plants, then these can be erected along the terracing.

Generally speaking the garden must be constructed from the bottom upwards, and not the reverse. If the ground slopes right to the roadway or boundary at the bottom, then in order to make the first terrace – which may be the lawn and patio – you will have to bank up the boundary line as you proceed with the excavated earth and then face it with wall, bricks or rocks.

If you have to build a retaining wall, however, you should sink into its face a drainage pipe, otherwise water which drains down the hillside will be trapped behind and may eventually lead to problems.

Always keep an eye open for the best way of disposing of excavated soil without carting it far, and remember that 1 sq. yd. of stone weighs about 2 cwt.

You can make some steepish grass banks if the soil is reasonably firm, turfed rather than sown, but they will need mowing with a hovering mower.

You need at least 6 in. of soil for grass and at least 1 ft. of soil for plants. Adequate terracing will be needed round the house to allow access to the greenhouse, garden shed and for the moving of garden materials, the provision of seating and so on.

The siting of small specimen conifers and foliage plants is particularly attractive in hillside gardens; they give that vital three dimensional effect. Trees, however, should generally be sited towards the top or to one side.

Ornamental features can be added as you progress and there are very many choices of materials. Cast concrete, slabs and stone laid in concrete, slabs laid on sand, broken slab paving, brick paths, asphalt and bitumen, blocks, bricks and dressed stone, screenblocks, drystones, cobbles, all have their merits.

Avoid using loose stones as these need a good deal of maintenance, especially when weeding.

If you have grassed banks then do not construct quick

changes in level, or steep humps or hollows, or mowing will cause scalping or missed parts.

The hillside and banks allow enormous scope for the establishment of mixed plantings of carpeting plants and low shrubs, with erect shrubs and small weeping trees here and there for accent and contrast.

Heathers, gorse, brooms, cistus, hypericums, dwarf conifers, Japanese maples and no end of other plants can be used. Remember that the plants can be just as attractive from below as above.

Rambler roses can look very effective pegged down on slopes, as can climbing roses tied to a low wooden trellis. Many other kinds of trailing and climbing plants lend themselves to being grown along the slope.

Hillside gardens should allow the maximum planting of climbers against fences and walls and on the house, and the free use of windowboxes and tubs and urns near the house can establish immediate interest from close range.

Generally put such features as tall walls, hedges, arches and pergolas towards the side of the slope – so as to allow a more or less complete view from top to bottom, broken only by the various compact features at each level.

Level terraces can, of course, be either paved or grassed, and provision should also be made for quite ambitious pools, fountains and waterfalls, and these are particularly enhanced on a hillside garden. Raised beds are also especially appropriate – linking one level to another and bordering pathways.

Hilltop Gardens. Planning and making a hilltop garden is one of the greatest tests of a gardener's ingenuity. The main priority is to provide shelter against gales for yourself and the plants in the garden. So the first job, after initial planning of the layout, is to establish trees and tall hedges and other kinds of windbreaks, such as wall bays for climbing plants.

It is not until later when such trees are becoming established that the main plantings of herbaceous plants, roses, shrubs and bulbs can take place, although naturally the time this can be done depends a lot on how exposed the actual location is in relation to the worst the local weather can do.

The first area to consider on a hilltop site is the area

A rock garden can make a colourful boundary between a patio and the lawn. Note the use of dwarf conifers to create interest in the winter months. *Photo Frank Hermann.*

surrounding the house. This should be sheltered with trees, or even a high wall if the weather can get too rough. If the hill slope is steep it may mean that you could only provide a flat area of ground on one or two sides.

Even if you have to construct it, this flat area is necessary because not only does it make the house stand out as a feature but it will provide sufficient level space for siting the greenhouse, garden shed, and patio, all of which need to be close to the house.

The patio will be a main feature, perhaps with a low cavity wall along it, planted with the most suitable plants of the season, and adequately shielded. And it can have, at the hillside end, an arch-covered ornamental gate, leading towards the next feature, the hillside garden.

Steps, curving or straight, will lead from the patio to the lawn,

Hydrangeas are among the most popular of late summer flowering shrubs. Many varieties produce blue flowers on acid soil, pink flowers on alkaline soil.

which, to accommodate the slope of ground, will probably have to be partly excavated at one side and perhaps built up at another. An ornamental retaining wall could be built at the junction of the patio with the lawn, and this can be planted with rock plants in cavities left for the purpose.

The lawn can still have the usual flower-beds in it or round it, with accentuating specimen trees and will presumably connect to a path leading to the hillside garden.

The hillside garden will have a path that winds through it and will pass through rock outcrops, partly made as planted rock gardens, rocky bluffs for carpeting or hanging plants and low conifers to contrast with the tall trees that will give the main shelter from gales in winter.

The actual summit, of course, will be the *pièce de résistance*. It will need to be partly clothed with trees and shrubs to keep off the wind, possibly to the south-west and the north and north-east, with views to the other points of the compass.

A short avenue of grass or steps, flanked by hydrangeas, conifers, or other plants, can lead to the hilltop itself, where, perhaps, you might like to site a flat circle of ornamental bricks or paving, with an island bed, and low walls round the edges with seating set in them.

The hillside garden and hilltop provide endless scope for sun-lovers and shade-loving plants. Heathers set in circles cut out of grassy slopes, and kept well trimmed after flowering, can be an especially bright feature most of the year.

If you wish to grow fruit and vegetables then these would best be sited somewhere in the shielded house-garden.

Retaining Walls. The materials available for walls are many. For low walls, of not more than two or three courses high, a light foundation of rubble tamped into the soil will be adequate.

But more generally in terracing, the wall is to be built in loose ground and you will need to dig down to provide a foundation of at least 3 in. of concrete. With taller walls, you will need a foundation of up to 6 in. of concrete, again set in the soil rather than on it, for terracing.

Where the wall is to retain a large amount of soil or hold back a fairly extensive terrace, you will certainly need a double course. A cheap brick or breeze block can be faced with the better quality material. The cavities along the top of the double walls can either be capped or filled with some of the wide variety of plants suited to this type of situation.

Where you have to dig into the soil for foundations, you will also need to insert a damp course about 6 in. above soil level. Weep holes for drainage are vital, too, and should be left at intervals of about 6 ft. along the base of the wall. To assist drainage on the retained side, crocks or cinders should be placed in the soil close to the weep holes.

Dry walls are generally not suitable for retaining walls on steep slopes, unless you are a real professional at building them. But you could try your hand at a low one for raised beds or a slight terrace effect. Dry walls more than 1 ft. high should be given a backward slant of about 1 in. to 1 ft. in height.

Tiny peat walls can also be most attractive for a low terrace but getting hold of the blocks may be difficult in some areas. They look best in rural settings or a garden with a slightly ragged look.

With solid walls, which are most suitable for terracing, the main points to remember are the absolute necessity of maintaining line, level and plumb. Adequate mortar joints and the need for piers or other forms of support are also vital in long walls that have to retain a large amount of soil.

Line level and plumb are assured by regularly checking with string line, spirit-level and plumb line.

For concrete blockwork, mortars made with ordinary cement and sand are too strong. Using slightly weaker mortar of masonry cement and builders' sand – not concreting sand – in a one to five proportion will ensure that any cracks that may develop through settlement or temperature changes will follow the mortar line and will not crack the blocks. Then, you can re-point as necessary. Mortar joints should be made about $\frac{3}{8}$ in. thick for blocks and the blocks should be laid to 'bond', with staggered vertical joints as with brickwork.

Steps in Terracing. There are numerous materials available, but for a difficult site the choice is fairly restricted – either completely flat-surfaced slabs or heavy timber.

In terracing, steps may have to be constructed from a fairly high drop and made in a way that they are entirely safe for pedestrians. From a high drop the steps should not be too steep; each step should have a few inches extra length than is normally the case, and with extra long flights and curving ones a regular 'landing' perhaps with a seat may be useful. The treads should not be less than about 16 in. and the risers about 6 in. Construct them from the bottom upwards.

Give some thought too to the wings of the steps particularly on hillside sites. These side walls can take a variety of attractive forms. You could use cavity walls for planting, peat walls, stone, or formal brickwork capped for finish. If you do decide on planting the walls lining your steps, do not use trailing plants which are likely to grow down to the steps themselves.

6 Cottage Gardens

Cottage Gardens. To many people, a cottage garden is simply a chaos of colourful plants. This conveys the general impression that there is no planning involved, and all you need do is sow seeds all over the place. The facts are very different. The successful cottage garden is invariably the outcome of careful observation.

The basic design of the original cottage garden was usually so simple as to be no design at all – merely a straight path from the gate to the front door with two plots on each side. But there would be certain features in many cottage gardens which would often dominate the scene.

An old gnarled apple tree – a Bramley Seedling, perhaps, or something similar – would be the largest single specimen. This would provide blossom in the spring, fruit for preserves and jellies, stewed apples for apple pies, and – a trick that sums up the cottage garden – a home for a climbing rose. Every inch of space was utilized, both on the ground and up in the air.

The art of topiary, clipping trees into peculiar shapes, came back to large gardens in the Victorian period with the revival of formalism. This, too, strayed over into the cottage gardens – a clipped hedge decorated with the occasional peacock, or large clipped specimens, either simple mounds of yew or box, perhaps with a figure on top, would be placed at an appropriate point to form a solid basis for the design. Similarly, there would be two or three large shrub roses or ornamental shrubs.

The rose bush might be the thornless 'Zephirine Drouhin', or

The modern version of the cottage garden. Here an old-brick path
is flanked by borders of apparently carelessly arranged plants.

Pinks are ideal plants for every garden. They will grow in any sunny
situation so long as the soil is not waterlogged.

the old large white, 'Frau Karl Drushki' or some long-forgotten hybrid – like the variety now known as 'Rubrotincta', a single damask rose with a white flower margined with red.

The shrub could be something very common – *Kerria japonica Flore Pleno*, known as the 'Jews' Mallow', or it could equally well be some little known, exotic plant – perhaps a hamamelis or a viburnum, given to the skilled cottage gardener as a cutting.

There is no catalogue of 'Cottage Garden Flowers'. Even so, there are certain plants that have come to be associated with the style, although it would be better to describe many of them as 'Tea-cosy' flowers, the sort that are seen on elementary embroidery designs and on coloured calendars.

Yet these do give the effect of old-world cottage gardens – hollyhocks, for example, are singularly appropriate, although now difficult to grow because of the prevalence of rust. Again, although of comparatively recent introduction, clarkia, godetia and nasturtium are easy annuals which give a good show, need little skill, and fit into the picture.

Curiously enough, there are some plants which will grow very well indeed in small gardens but are totally unsuccessful in larger areas where they might be somewhat lost. The Madonna Lily (*Lilium andidum*) is the best example, for it only grows really well in a small space.

Sunflowers, the big brash yellow 'frying-pan' annual types, are also typical – because the seed can be put to good use. It should also be remembered that the runner bean was grown originally as a decorative plant – and tripods of scarlet runners are very much in the cottage garden tradition. So, too, are sweet peas, both the annual kind and the everlasting pea.

The old-time cottager realized the decorative value of vegetables. The beautiful glaucous foliage of nearly all the brassicas – the cabbages, cauliflowers, sprouting broccoli and so on – is attractive if regarded with an eye that has not been conditioned by false values of rarity.

These are some of the elements of the cottage garden. But it is not something that can be ordered, ready made, from a landscape gardener. It must depend entirely on the thought, care, concentration and skill of the owner. But – given that – it is one of the most beautiful and satisfactory styles of gardening in the world.

88

7 Labour Saving Gardens

It is quite possible to make a trouble-free, light-work garden of pleasing design. Most of the basic garden design principles that have already been mentioned will still apply. You will still want, no doubt, a patio, lawns, a selection of trees and shrubs. The problem is to substitute less troublesome features for those that require year-round maintenance.

Larger paved areas than would normally be the case can help and choice of materials will also affect the amount of work required through the year. Gravel paths for example, require regular maintenance. Slabs, asphalt or concrete do not.

Pools can be left to their own devices for long periods of the year and require only occasional tending; huge rockeries can be tedious, but again the amount of work they will entail is largely controlled by the type of plants you use. Lawns are trouble free for five months of the year, apart from regular raking of dead leaves; but for the remaining seven months they will require a good deal of time-consuming attention.

Perhaps the major part of the work in a pleasing design can be eliminated by careful selection of plants for borders and beds. The conventional plantings of geraniums, salvias, antirrhinums, petunias, lobelia, etc., involve much work in growing, planting out and general maintenance. Try this arrangement as a trouble-free substitute: plant out dwarf shrubs like lavenders, heathers, potentiallas, cotoneasters, dwarf conifers, helianthemums and

There is nothing to beat bedding plants for creating a riot of sheer colour in the summer. Most of the plants shown here need to be over-wintered in a frost-free shed.

set them out 2 to 3 ft. apart. In between them, plant a selection of winter, summer and autumn flowering bulbs. In the centre of the bed, plant three or four clematis, choosing varieties to flower at different times of the year; but don't give them any support. Just let them grow along the ground, spreading between the shrubs and pegging down where necessary. You will have a year-round colour spectacular that is hard to beat and, apart from one or two clean-up operations, it is entirely work-free.

There are many other ground cover shrubs that can be used

Some ferns, like the *Blechnum tabulare* shown here have all the bold architectural qualities so popular in modern gardens. This one is evergreen and makes excellent ground cover.

for planting a less-work border, including *Cytisus procumbens*, a mat of bright yellow flowers in May; *Euonymus fortunei* 'Gracilis', a spreading green foliage with silver-grey variegated leaves; *Genista dalmatica*, a carpet of white yellow summer flowers; *Juniperus procumbens* 'Nana', a low-growing conifer; *Vinca major* 'Elegantissima'; *Senecio laxifolius* with its grey leaves.

Ground cover perennials which are suitable for in-filling between larger shrubs, thus creating labour-saving borders, include: ajuga, bergenia, hosta, polygonum, pulmonaria, *Sedum spectabile*, *Stachys lanata* and *Tiraella cordifolia*.

Consider all these when planning your borders.

Colour Planner for Heathers

TYPE	VARIETY	HEIGHT (in.)	FLOWER COLOUR	FOLIAGE COLOUR	SEASON
Erica Cinerea (Bell Heather)	Alba Major	12	white	bright green	
	Atro Sanguinea	12	red	green	
	Apple Blossom	9	lilac-pink	green	
	C. Eason	9	red	deep-green	
	Cevennes	9	mauve-pink	green	June–Oct.
	Golden Drop	6	deep pink	golden/red in winter	
	J. Eason	9	salmon	bronze	
	P. Patrick	12	purple	green	
	Velvet Night	12	deepest claret	green	
Erica Hybrids	Dawn	9	rose bells	green	
	H. Maxwell	12	rose bells	green	
	Gwen	9	lilac bells	green	June–Oct.
	F. White	9	white bells	green	
	Stuartii	12	pink, tipped red	bright green	
	Williamsii	9	pink	fresh green	
E. tetralix (Cross-leaved Heather)	Alba Mollis	9	white	frosty-grey	
	C. Underwood	12	red	green	June–Sept.
	Hookstone Pink	12	pink	silver	
	L. Underwood	9	orange-pink	green	
	Pink Star	9	pink	grey	
Calluna vulgaris (Ling)	Alba Plena	14	white	green	
	Alportii	24	wine-red	green	
	Barnett Anley	24	purple	green	
	Blaze Away	18	mauve	orange/red/flame	
	Beoley Gold	18	white	golden	
	Cuprea	12	purple	copper	July–Sept.
	Elsie Purnell	20	*double* pink	green	
	Foxii Nana	3	purple	moss-green	
	Golden Feather	18	seldom flowers	golden-orange	
	Joy Vanstone	18	pink	golden	

92

Colour Planner for Heathers

TYPE	VARIETY	HEIGHT (in.)	FLOWER COLOUR	FOLIAGE COLOUR	SEASON
	Orange Queen	24	pink	golden to orange	
	Multicolor	12	magenta	yellow/orange/red	
	Robert Chapman	18	lilac	bronze/red	July–Sept.
	Sister Ann	3	pink	silver	
	Sunset	12	pink	flecked yellow/orange	
	Tib	12	red-purple	green	
Erica Carnea (Mountain Heather)	Aurea	8	pink	golden	Feb.–April
	Cecilia Beale	9	white	green	Dec.–Mar.
	Eileen Porter	6	rich red	green	Oct.–April
	King George	7	rose-red	green	Jan.–April
	Loughrigg	8	purple	blue-green/bronze	Feb.–Mar.
	Pink Pearl	7	shell pink	pale green	Feb.–April
	Pirbright Rose	8	bright pink	green	Feb.–April
	Praecox Rubra	6	deep red	deep green	Dec.–Mar.
	Ruby Glow	6	deep red	green	Mar.–May
	Startler	8	coral pink	green	Feb.–Mar.
	Springwood White	7	white	green	Feb.–April
	Springwood Pink	6	pink	green	Feb.–April
	Vivelii	6	rich red	purple-green	Feb.–May
Erica darlyensis	type	24	rosy-mauve	green	Dec.–April
	A. Johnson	24	deep pink	green	Dec.–April
	Furzey	24	purple-pink	bronze	Feb.–May
	G. Rendall	15	pink	green	Feb.–May
	J. Brummage	24	pink	yellow/orange	Feb.–May
	Silver Beads	18	white	green	Dec.–Mar.
Erica Mediterranea (Spring Heather)	Brightness	24	red	green	
	Glauca	30	pale pink	blue-grey	
	Coccinea	30	rose-purple	green	
	type	36	pink	green	Mar.–May
	type Superba	60	pink	green	
	type Nana Alba	18	white	pale green	
	W. Rackliffe	24	large white	bright green	

▲ Dwarf brooms are a blaze of sheer colour in early spring. The one shown here, *Cytisis praecox* has primrose yellow flowers.

Dwarf evergreen azaleas flower so profusely you literally cannot see the leaves. Like rhododendrons, they need an acid soil. ▲

The Heather Garden. Heathers are suited to most gardens as labour savers, particularly as they have collectively such long flowering seasons, which planned carefully can mean year-round colour.

They need little attention and grow into neat, colourful hummocks or form a mat growth which smothers weeds. For these reasons they look well as specimens or in mass, on flat ground or sloping sites, on cliffs and rock outcrops. Suitable, in fact, for almost any type of garden. They can be set formally into geometrically shaped beds or planted in a complete heather garden, graduated according to height, season of flowering, foliage and colour.

They can be mixed with rock-garden plants, put among shrubs where they are invaluable for low growing carpeting, or be grown as individual specimens. They are also most suited for island beds, highlighting perhaps a specimen tree or shrub.

Most heathers put up with a wide range of soil, though it must be acid or neutral. *Erica arborea, australis, mediterranea, carnea, lustanica, multiflora, terminalis and x darlyensis* withstand alkaline soils.

Most tolerate moist soil but it should be well drained. Both clay and light soil should have plenty of organic matter incorporated – a little well-rotted manure, but mainly peat, leaf-mould and garden compost.

94

Paving is being used more and more in modern gardens. It looks best when several different colours and textures are used.

The hard lines of paving can be broken by leaving spaces where small plants can be grown. These create an air of informality.

These materials should also be forked in annually in the spring. In limy soils, it is best to make a raised bed for heathers so that a wide variety can be grown, filling the bed with a mixture of the bulky organic materials and retaining it with peat blocks – which slowly decay – or with stone blocks, which are permanent.

Generally fairly close planting of young plants is best, rather than using semi-mature plants which may not get over transplanting very well – unless from containers.

Compact types can be set about 7 to 12 in. apart, medium compact varieties 1 ft. to 18 in. apart, and tallish kinds 18 to 24 in. apart – with tall bush forms about half their height between.

On alkaline soils, feed in the spring with sequestrols but otherwise fertilizers or plant foods are unnecessary.

Heathers depend on their freedom of flowering, the compact kinds particularly, on light pruning or clipping after flowering, so new shoots grow in abundance, though there is a division of thought between people who claim that pruning should allow varying lengths of growth to give a clumpy form, or whether clipping should shape them into neat hummocks. Summer-flowering kinds are clipped in spring.

Calluna is what people commonly call heather. It is a low-growing, hummock-type plant, hates lime, stands exposed positions in full sun or partial shade and comes in varying leaf and flower colours. Main flowering period is late summer. 'Golden Feather' has bright golden-orange foliage, 'Robert Chapman' has reddish foliage, and 'Foxii Nana' is dark green and miniature in stature.

Daboecia has small bell-shaped flowers, is again hummock forming, not very hardy so appreciates a sheltered site, hates lime, does not mind damp soil and flowers from June to October. There is a wide variety of flower and leaf colour.

Erica is the genus with the widest variety of colours; many species are of hummock kind of heather, with numerous tiny blossoms, dense in growth. *E. carnea* is a very comprehensive compact species, all sorts of varieties, able to stand lime, very hardy, flowering from October to April in its very many forms. *E. mediterranea* is a tall grown shrub, flowering in spring; and it does not mind stony ground. One of the hardiest of all heathers is *E. tetralix*, a compact type, hating lime, but not minding damp. It flowers from June until October. Bell heather is *E. cinerea.*

One of the best of the medium-compact kinds is *E. x darlyensis*, smothered in blossom from December until April. It is available in a variety of forms. The tallest of all is *E. arborea*, which in mild localities can grow to 20 ft. tall. However, it does not stand hard winters, so needs a sheltered site in normal parts. It flowers in March and April and there is a golden-leaved form.

Heathers are particularly attractive in winter, with their various foliage colours and always brighten up the coldest months, peeping through the snow when in flower.

In the spring and summer they are excellent for bees and butterflies and generally can be increased by layering or short summer cuttings of green shoots.

Trouble-Free Conifers. The increased emphasis on labour-saving plants these days has brought a new interest in dwarf conifers. The work involved is negligible after initial planting since they are not fussy about soil. The poorer the soil, the longer they remain dwarfs. They are rarely troubled by pests and diseases.

But most forms of dwarfs are dignified little plants and hate being made to look ridiculous by thoughtless planting, under large trees for example.

Probably the best place for them is where natural scenic beauty already exists, or where it has been artificially created in miniature. They will fit in perfectly with these surroundings, giving the impression of age and maturity that is associated with trees, yet in scale with adjacent materials.

Dwarf conifers are perhaps best used as a specific feature, rather than dotted in various parts of the garden. Plan your groups carefully so that you get the best from a wide range of colour, size habit and even texture. Take into account the winter colours which with some species are different from the summer.

Pay attention to backgrounds, so that they are not over-shadowed by other, taller garden subjects. With dwarfs, one really appreciates them better when they can be fully seen. Careful siting is important. None of them likes draughts – as distinct from winds – and over-dry conditions will also affect them for a year or two after planting.

The list of varieties available is endless. Some of the conical or globose forms are excellent when used in isolation on a small lawn or in tubs on the patio while the prostrate, mat-forming qualities of the junipers make them excellent ground-cover plants, particularly for covering banks or difficult ground.

For greater versatility, many types thrive in pots and thus have the advantage of portability.

Paved Gardens. Raw concrete should definitely not be used for covering any major area of the garden. It is far too per-manent. The best choice for paved gardens is coloured slabs. A large expanse of paving will tend to throw up the colours and it is wise to choose the more subdued colours.

Crazy paving can also be used but again this tends to be a rather permanent arrangement in view of the amount of con-crete and base materials that will be needed to firm the area off.

Paved gardens are particularly suitable for smaller town gardens, or for front gardens with an island cut out for planting; or it can replace a lawn in the planning scheme of a larger garden and still blend pleasantly with an overall design scheme.

The design of your paved garden will naturally be an open one with perhaps several areas of ground left unpaved for island beds of shrubs and conifers, according to overall dimensions.

▲ Simplicity is the keynote of this garden, which is laid out simply to trees and lawn. Such design can be very restful.

A corner of a garden with flowering shrubs and conifers tumbling ▲ over the paving make a romantic retreat.

You can also have a wide range of containers and container-grown specimens.

It is still worth leaving a fair expanse of border around the paved area if this is possible so that you can plant out trees and shrubs that will clothe unsightly walls and fences and give your garden some outline and depth. If a border is not possible, revert back to container-grown subjects, which can be used for similar effect.

Crazy paving is more suited to shaping and informality, though this must be a matter of choice, bearing in mind the permanence of most forms of crazy paving.

The design possibilities are really endless but, as with all other types of garden design, try to establish a central feature that will act as a focal point. There are numerous other tricks, such as leaving out the odd slab here and there and planting the ground with heathers or herbs; creating terraces – even artificial ones – to get away from the entirely flat outlook and using tiny edging walls in a material that blends with the choice of paving either capped or built with a cavity for planting.

There is no reason why the gardener who chooses a paved garden cannot grow fruit trees and set up a mini-orchard.

You don't need exotic plants to create a colourful effect. All the plants in this attractive small rock garden are very ordinary but very effective. *Photo Frank Herrmann.*

Obviously, this will be possible with cordon fruit in any borders; or the trees can be grown in pots.

Pots should always be lagged with straw or other suitable material during winter so that the roots do not get frozen. The trees you buy should be four-year-old bushes or pyramids on dwarfing stock. Apples and pears are particularly amenable to this form of culture and you might like to try others, such as greengages, plums, peaches and nectarines.

Place apples and pears in the less favourable situations of your garden, saving the warmer area for the choicer fruits such as greengages and peaches. The number of plants you can grow in small areas is surprising. You will need little more than 1 sq. yd. of floor space to accommodate each tree.

Don't let the trees bear too much fruit in the first two years. Turn out the fruit spurs as they develop. Established pot-grown trees will need re-potting every two or three years.

'Just Lawn and Trees'. Another labour saving arrangement that can be adapted to almost any size of garden is one in which the basic ingredients are simply grass, trees and shrubs.

The garden would take the form of a pleasant glade which would be reached from a fairly wide patio at the rear of the house. The glade would be a wholly lawned area in which islands had been cut out for the siting of individual specimen subjects. The front part of the lawn would be left open, apart from a pair of conifers or standard roses on each side of the opening leading from the patio to the lawn.

Then, there could be an informal arrangement of trees and shrubs, with the smaller, low-growing and prostrate subjects at the front allowing the outline to rise gently down the garden.

There are many subjects suitable for this sort of plan. But avoid any trees that will grow to huge proportions, over-shadowing the remaining members of your glad family. At the front you could use groups of heathers, hydrangeas, hypericum, banking up with magnolia, cherry, crab apple, buddleia, *Pieris japonica*, Japanese maple, Chinese juniper and so on.

Around the base of each tree, cut out a bed that is the width of the branch span of the tree, since grass will not grow well underneath. The bed can be underplanted with suitable subjects, if you wish, such as seasonal bulbs.

8 Lawns

The beauties of a lawn are so self-evident that few people ever stop to ask themselves what a lawn's purpose is. In fact there are several points that combine to make a lawn one of the most important features of any garden. In the first place it is green, the most restful colour in the whole spectrum: it is also a way of creating vistas. Not only can the lawn lead the eye away to beds and borders and distant trees, it can be the perfect foil for features within it. Bulbs planted in the lawn will not interfere with mowing, if they are kept to one corner. Specimen trees; it can be the perfect foil for features within it when planted in a lawn. Isolated beds in formal patterns and shapes set in a lawn are extremely effective if well kept and carefully edged. On the other hand curved edges, provided they are not too sharp, are easier to mow particularly with motor mowers, and curving lawn edges may be used for those eye-leading effects or just to break up a long monotonous straight line.

Your lawn will probably combine several uses. Its shape and position will be decided also by such considerations as the lay-out of paths and access to other parts of the garden. It will be planned to take account of the positions of established trees, the view from the house and road, rock-garden features, ornaments, slopes and levels and the size of the garden as a whole.

The first thing to appreciate about a lawn is that it is composed of living, growing plants that need just as much care and attention as any other living, growing plant.

Many of the troubles which affect lawns can be avoided through preparation of the site, which should always be done properly even if the ground has already been cultivated. It is always much more difficult to correct a badly made lawn than to see that the soil and drainage conditions are correct in the first place.

The preparations for making a lawn, whether by turfing or seeding, are roughly the same. If the site is at a new house the effects of the builders' work including debris and disturbed sub-soil must be removed before a start can be made. A regular 6-in. layer of top-soil will be needed for the finished lawn, and on sites that have been cleared by the builders it may be necessary to buy in soil. Such soil may also be used to achieve a level grade, as it is likely to make for irregular growth if you denude one area of soil in order to fill up a hollow in another. When constructing terraces or making other changes involving considerable movements of earth it is best to remove the top-soil altogether, make the required levels with the sub-soil and then return the top-soil. Levels are easily made by laying a straight edge with spirit-level on pegs set into the ground at convenient intervals.

Good drainage is essential to a lawn, and according to the heaviness and stickiness of the soil and sub-soil you should consider whether land tile draining pipes may be necessary, either in the form of a single pipeline or with lateral pipes stemming from the main pipeline, which empties into a soakaway, or preferably a drain.

Ideally, after the preliminary digging, the ground should be allowed to over-winter. This helps to settle the soil and leaves it ready to work in the drier spring weather. However, most gardeners like to get on with tasks once started and by hoeing and raking they will break up the clods and level the surface while keeping an eagle eye out for weeds. Going over the ground with the heel of your boot to feel out and consolidate soft spots is known as 'heeling'. There is no real need to use a heavy roller; a light roller such as may be found on the back of

Simplicity is the keynote of this bedding scheme, and that's what makes it so effective. Red, white and purple flowers contrast with plants with silver or bronze foliage.

modern hand mowers should be all that is needed. During the soil preparation the surface may be improved with plenty of sand (builder's sand is cheap if not perfect) if the soil is heavy, or peat and well-rotted compost if the land is light. Peat may also be included with the sand on heavy soils. Almost any amount of sand or grit, and peat at 7 lb. per sq. yd. will be suitable for heavy clay, and over 14 lb. per sq. yd. of manure or well-rotted compost and the same amount of peat will help light soils. A proprietary lawn fertilizer may also be added at this stage. When you have raked and double-raked and gently firmed out every bump and hollow you are ready to sow or turf.

Turf or Seed. The great advantage of turf is that it gets off to a quicker start than seed. Late autumn and winter (when no frost is about) are the best times for turfing. It can be done in the spring if there is not too much drought, and even in the summer provided mechanical water spraying is kept going almost permanently during the day in dry weather. Turf is simple to lay, requires less fine preparation of the soil and is usually more robust against the ravages of weather, disease and garden pests, such as birds. Despite these advantages, seed is cheaper and easy to obtain at high quality. There is a British Standard for turf, but even the most excellent turf will deteriorate in places where it was not intended to grow. Seed sowing is limited to the period August–September, to spring or even early summer when the dangers of drought and competition from weeds are greater.

Turfing. When ordering turves ask for the names of the grasses they contain. These should be fine quality bents and fescues for an ornamental lawn. They should be free of weeds and disease. If not regularly $1\frac{1}{2}$ in. thick, put them upside down in a box of standard thickness and slice off the extra soil with a two-handed shear or a carving knife.

Turves may come in 1-sq.-ft. sizes, or 1 ft. × 2 ft., or 1 ft. × 3 ft. Do not pile them but keep them flat until laid. Keep in mind the pattern made by bricks in a wall when laying turves and you will not go wrong. Do not forget to rake in a final dressing of a compound fertilizer before laying the turves, and use planks to prevent heavy treading on the newly laid lawn.

Start from a corner of the site. Use a garden line for straight sections and cut curving edges with a half-moon edger once the turf is laid, using a hosepipe to give good, graceful curves. Make sure the turves are set as close together as possible and water and topdress with sandy soil afterwards to fill in gaps between turves. Hollows should be filled up with this top-dressing, and mounds levelled by removing soil under the turves. Further top-dressings may be given when growth begins and the regular programme of maintenance is being followed.

Seeding. A finer tilth is needed for seeding and a complete garden fertilizer must be mixed with the raked soil a few days beforehand. Grass seed can be bought ready-mixed or you can mix your own. You will need about 2 oz. to the sq. yd. and some in reserve for areas that may need to be reseeded.

Some special dwarf varieties of grass are now available which require less mowing. The following are suggested for various types of lawn. In general, the best grasses, fescues and bents, germinate more slowly than rye grass or meadow grass.

Parts by weight

Top quality lawns	4 Chewings' Fescue 1 Browntop Bent	(American or New Zealand varieties)
Children's play lawn	6 S 23 Perennial Ryegrass 3 Crested Dogstail 1 Browntop Burnt	(Ryegrass must be mown regularly or it becomes inordinately tough)
For shady places	6 Chewings' Fescue or Creeping Red Fescue 3 Smooth-stalked Meadow Grass 1 Crested Dogstail	

Before sowing, rake the site so that the tiny furrows will catch the seed. You can soak the seed in a mild solution of antiseptic to

Belladonna lilies *Amaryllis belladonna* and *Zephyranthes candida* make perfect companions for growing at the foot of a south wall in well drained soil.

put off birds and mix it with sand to make distribution easier. A distributor may be used, or use rods or lines to divide the site into square yards and sow by hand. The seed should be lightly raked in after sowing, traversing the lines of the original raking. Do not roll until the seedlings have developed. Do not expect germination for 10 to 20 days. When the grass reaches 2 in. high mow it with the blades set about 1 in. high. When the grass is established this can be reduced to about $\frac{3}{4}$ in. for hardy lawns and $\frac{1}{2}$ in. for top-quality lawns.

Watch out for weeds or alien grasses and remove them while small without disturbing the sown grass. A dressing of good John Innes type compost may be given after two or three months, though this should not be strictly necessary if the lawn site was properly prepared.

Tools for Lawn Maintenance

HAND MOWERS. Really all that is needed unless the lawn area exceeds 50 sq. yd. or unless you are a lawn enthusiast who wishes to cut the lawn at least twice a week in May and June (which is good practice, by the way) is a simple hand mower. Hand mowers are of two types: the roller and sidewheel. The roller type has a rear roller and another roller in the front which

Even the most unpromising town garden can be turned into an oasis of colour and peacefulness. Note the use made of the walls, and the retention of the open centre in the form of a lawn.

together ensure that the blades follow closely the surface of the lawn and so give a close neat cut. The sidewheel roller has two large wheels on either side of the cutter and a small roller at the rear. It is lighter and more adapted to cutting rough grass.

POWERED CYLINDER MOWERS. These have similar curved blades to hand mowers, which form a cylinder and cut against a bottom plate, but are powered by petrol engines, batteries or mains electricity. Powered machines are easily able to cut a wider swathe than human effort alone will allow, so the blades may be 14 in. or 18 in. wide compared to the conventional 12-in. hand mower. Electrically powered mowers are simple to operate, quiet and do not produce exhaust gases. They are probably better for smaller lawns. You will also need a hand mower for odd corners and verges where grit and stones might adversely affect the motor mower blades.

ROTARY MOWERS. Rotary mowers, powered by petrol, batteries or mains electricity, are marvellous for dealing with areas of rough and longer grass. The rotary mower has a horizontal blade which whirls round and chops off the heads of everything that comes within its compass. The speed at which the blade rotates provides its cutting effectiveness and 100 cuts a yard produces a better finish than 50 cuts a yard. The newest type of

107

rotary mower runs on the 'hovercraft' principle and has the special merit of making a close cut and following undulations and banks easily, and dissecting the grass into myriads of tiny fragments so that no collecting box is needed for the mown grass.

EDGE TRIMMERS. Shears are the cheapest edgers and rely not so much on the sharpness of the blade as the perfection of the scissor-like mating of the two blades. The long-handled blades that make a vertical cut are the most useful, although there are types adapted to cutting horizontally. You can also buy electrically operated trimmers with oscillating teeth. Aids to edge trimming include the half-moon blade which will enable you to recut edges that have lost their definition, and both plastic and metal strip will help to consolidate an edge once it is defined.

DISTRIBUTORS AND SPREADERS. Ranging from knapsack to wheeled designs, these are excellent for distributing fertilizers and solid weedkillers evenly in powder or liquid form.

SPRINKLERS. Most lawn enthusiasts end up buying automatic hose-attached water sprinklers. These should only be used in relation to an outside standpipe for which water authority permission is needed, and watering is restricted at times of drought. Extra water is usual; a few days' drought will affect delicate lawn constitutions.

AERATORS AND DRAINERS. Scarifiers are very useful for freeing the grass from moss and other impediments. The 'Springbok' fork, consisting of springy powerful wires, is most useful. Aerating the soil becomes important when it gets too compact, and special hollow-tined forks working on the soil will pull out core-like 'moon-rock' samples, leaving it free for both air, water and fertilizer. Spiked rollers achieve the same effect.

If you inherit an old lawn it is possible to renovate it without digging it up. Simply water it with a contact weedkiller (paraquat-diquat) and the top growth will die off within a few days in sunny weather without the weedkiller affecting the soil beneath. After about a week proceed as though aerating it. Do this thoroughly, leaving holes every few inches and remove the cores to the compost heap. Brush in a mixture of gypsum and well-matured compost which has been sieved. If the land is heavy increase the proportion of gypsum, making it say 2 to 1 by bulk; if the soil is light increase the proportion of compost (powdered seaweed can also be used). Grass likes a soil which is on the acid side but not too acid which it may be if it has been used for a lawn for a long time. Test the soil for acid and if you find it much below pH 6·5 (see soil-testing) add a little ground limestone to the mixture up to 4 oz per sq. yd. Sand or peat can be added to the mixture according to whether the soil is heavy or light. Work it well into the holes in the soil and then scarify to get rid of the old grass roots. The surface should then be thinly covered with a mixture of sand and peat with ordinary lawn fertilizer in the prescribed quantity. Lightly rake and sow the seed of your choice.

Diseases

FUSARIUM PATCH. Patches of yellowing dead grass sometimes appear in summer but most often in spring and autumn under conditions of excessive moisture. The patches growing up to a foot in size eventually join up and should be immediately treated with Bordeaux mixture combined with malachite green dye, but encourage healthy turf and do not overfeed with sulphate of ammonia.

CORTICUM. The grass becomes discoloured like straw with tiny red threads appearing on the grass blades. It is a late-summer to autumn occurrence and may be treated with Bordeaux/malachite green.

FAIRY RINGS. Circles of exceptionally green grass may develop due to the action of certain fungi which feed on the soil, not the grass. They are difficult to eradicate chemically and the only remedy otherwise is to dig out and returf.

Pests

WORMS. It seems a pity that the better the lawn the more likely worms are to appear, because they aerate the soil with their burrowing and create humus. They are a serious problem in large numbers, however, and mowrah meal, derris and potassium permanganate are some of the eradicants recommended.

LEATHER JACKETS. In small numbers these daddy-long-legs larvae will not be too harmful, but if the lawn is severely affected BHC dust may be used in late autumn.

ANTS. Chlordane is effective against these not very frequent troublers.

Autumn colour is the last great bonus of the gardener's year. Such trees look most effective against a background of evergreens.

Cyclamen neapolitanum flowers from August to October, the flowers coming out of the bare soil before the leaves emerge.

9 Fences, Hedges, Paths and Edgings

Fences, hedges, paths and edgings, together with drives and steps, all serve essentially utilitarian functions: pergolas, patios and garden walls, also included in this chapter, are less functional.

It is always important to try to relate the design of a drive or pathway, as well as the materials used, to the overall design of the garden. When it comes to planning a patio or drive, let your taste be the ultimate arbiter in the style and choice of materials. Before making up your mind what to do, see what other people have done, and don't be afraid of being eclectic. If you use styles and materials you like, the chances are that they will harmonize.

Drives. Gravel when properly laid and maintained is probably the most attractive material for drives, and it has the advantage of being inexpensive to lay and to maintain. It is important to stress that the gravel must be laid properly. The object is to achieve a firm surface that will not become a clayey quagmire in wet weather, that will not develop potholes, and that will not walk into the house when dry. The first essential is a good foundation. This should be made of a layer about six inches deep of builder's rubble or ashes, well compacted. On normal soils this will provide all the drainage that is needed for a gravel drive, but on soggy soils 3-in. drainage pipes should be laid in a herring-bone pattern at a depth of 6 in. When the gravel is laid it should be raked and rolled until a firm, even texture has been achieved. The main disadvantage of gravel is that weeds can grow in it, but this really is not a problem as they can easily be controlled by one of the persistent weedkillers.

Many people prefer drives with firmer surfaces, such as asphalt or tarmac mainly because they believe they are longer-lasting and need less maintenance. If this is to be so, they need to be laid as carefully as gravel. When tarmac or asphalt drives are laid over old gravel drives it is important that all loose chippings should be scraped off the surface of the old drive, that the surface should be re-levelled, and that persistent weeds should be killed before the new surface is laid. Both tarmac and asphalt should be laid at least 1 in. thick. The main difference between tarmac and asphalt is that tarmac is laid cold and is porous, whereas asphalt is laid hot and is not porous. Weeds are more likely to come up through tarmac than asphalt. In either case it is important to see that the drive is properly levelled and cambered. Unless this is done puddles will form on asphalt drives, and frost will quickly break up the surface of tarmac drives. Gaps should be left in the edgings for water to drain away into lawns or borders.

Concrete drives are long-lasting, but many people find the glaring white of untreated concrete unattractive: in addition such drives are relatively expensive to lay. They should be placed on a solid foundation of hardcore, and the concrete should be laid 4 in. thick. A more attractive and economic proposition is to lay the concrete in two parallel strips for the wheels of the car to go along, and possibly to use some contrasting material for the strip in the middle and at each side. Grass is unsuitable for this strip, as oil drips would soon kill patches and make it unattractive, but pebbles or setts embedded in a weak mortar, loose granite chippings or larger chunks of random sandstone are all practicable and attractive alternatives. Another possibility is to lay a herring-bone pattern of bricks between the strips of concrete, and to use parallel rows of paving slabs instead of the concrete.

Paths. The basic principles of constructing garden paths are similar to those for drives, but scaled down. The layer of hardcore need not be so deep, and if concrete is used, it need be laid

Top left Red hot pokers make a stunning feature in the herbaceous border late in summer. *Top right Amelanchier canadensis,* is a small shrubby tree with coppery spring growths, white flowers in early summer, red fruits and excellent autumn colour. *Bottom left* One of the modern lily hybrids. These are far easier to grow than most people realise. *Bottom right* Day lilies make a wonderful show, flowering continuously for about three months. *Opposite* striking effects in the herbaceous border.

only 2 in. thick. It is seldom advisable to make a garden path less than 3 ft. wide, and 4 ft. is usually better if you can afford the space. This width allows for the passage of wheel-barrows, lawn-mowers and other garden implements, as well as for the temporary intrusion of pathside plants: it is always a shame to have to cut back one of these plants just as it is coming into flower, merely because it is obstructing a pathway. Except in very large gardens where special visual effects may be needed, there is seldom any point in constructing paths wider than 4 ft. In general paths should be level with the ground on either side of them, except of course, where they divide raised beds of a rockery from, for example, a lawn. They should also be flat rather than cambered, as this makes them more comfortable to walk along.

Where gravel is used a foundation of 3 to 4 in. is adequate on most soils, but on heavy land the foundation needs to be 6 in. deep, and on really badly drained land 3-in. drainage pipes should be laid in herring-bone pattern at 18-in. intervals. A layer of gravel 2 in. thick is sufficient. Concrete, when used for a garden path, looks utilitarian and it is usually preferable to try to find some alternative material. Bricks laid in herring-bone pattern look particularly attractive, but the bricks must be sound or they will quickly be broken up by frost. There is a tendency for brick paths in shaded situations to become slippery: the slipperiness is caused by algae: it is a hazard that can easily be cured by watering with a proprietary algicide. Other brick-like materials can also be used to make attractive garden paths. Stable floor bricks, which have grooves in them for drainage, are attractive and can usually be bought inexpensively from demolition contractors, as can old limestone cobbles or granite setts, both of which make exceptionally attractive paths. When creating brick, cobble or granite sett paths it is best to lay a foundation of hardcore and then a 1-in. layer of concrete. Once this has been allowed to go off another 1-in. layer of weak mortar should be laid, and the bricks or setts embedded in this. Afterwards the bricks or setts can be pointed with a strong cement mixture, or earth can be used and grass allowed to grow up between the bricks. If this is the intention, extra care must be taken in getting the path level, otherwise it will be almost impossible to take the mower over it.

Paths do not necessarily need to be solid or continuous. Often 'stepping stones' in the lawn or through a rockery are just as serviceable. Paving slabs, which can be either of the old stone type or of the modern composition type, are the easiest materials for paths of this kind, but there are alternatives. If the stepping stones are required in the lawn, all that is necessary is to take out the turf to a sufficient depth, put in plywood shuttering, and lay the concrete *in situ*. Slabs made by this method can be rectangular, circular or irregular in shape. A similar type of stepping-stone path can be laid between borders, simply placing the stepping stones on the bare earth. It is important that the ground should be thoroughly weeded and dug, and then allowed to settle before the path is laid. Random stone flags make the most attractive paths of this type. Once laid the earth between the flags can be kept clean of weeds by the use of foliar weedkillers, or creeping plants allowed to establish themselves between the flags.

Crazy paving is probably the most popular of all materials for paths. Again, either stone or composition paving can be used: both are long lasting, though stone is more expensive. To make a lasting path, crazy paving should be laid on a firm foundation of rubble and concrete, embedded in mortar and pointed with a strong cement. If spot plants are to be grown between the paving slabs, holes should be left in the concrete foundation for drainage.

Steps. Steps are needed wherever a path passes from one level to another, and frequently to provide a means of transition from one level of a garden to another. It is usual to construct the step from the same material as that used for the path, and where the steps do not occur in a path the choice of materials remains much the same. The important thing about steps is that each step should be level: steps that slope away from you as you walk down them are lethal, particularly in wet weather. If they cover a large enough area to warrant a slope so that surface water will run off, the slope should be sideways, and a drop of $\frac{1}{2}$ in. in 6 ft. is adequate.

Edgings. Though they are unfashionable, edgings are still desirable in some situations, as for example, to separate a border

Water and sculpture have been features of every well-made garden since earliest times. No garden is complete without one or other, preferably both.

A patio in the modern idiom using different types of paving and pierced wall screens.

from a gravel path or drive. There are a number of possible materials that can be used. Concrete, though not the most attractive, is one of the most widely used. It is serviceable and long-lasting, though harsh to the eye in gardens that are in other ways mellow. Concrete edging can be bought in 4- or 5-ft. pre-cast lengths, with rounded edges on the surface that will be above ground. These pre-cast lengths need to be set in a base of concrete. Far more attractive in most gardens is brick, but the bricks need to be sound and hard. The bricks can either be laid horizontally as they are in walls, in which case they will need to be laid on a narrow foundation and cemented together with mortar, or they can be laid diagonally, or inserted vertically. Whichever style is adopted, trouble must be taken to ensure that, where they are to be laid in a straight line, that the line really is straight and preferably level. This is most easily done by using a line and spirit-level and driving pegs into the ground beside the line of edging to the desired height. It is usually best to use mortar when laying a brick edging.

Tiles of the type once fashionable in kitchen gardens make attractive edgings. They come in a variety of colours and patterns, but are usually of unglazed dark grey brick, either crenellated or with a barley-sugar twist along the top. The easiest way of laying them is to take out a shallow trench, vertical on one side only, kept straight by means of a board, place the tiles in

Lenten roses are excellent plants for a garden that suffers from too much shade. They flower for months on end and will seed themselves freely.

position and then lay a layer of concrete along the exposed side. Stone slabs, faced on one edge only, also make an attractive informal edging, and should be laid in a similar fashion.

Wood edgings are sometimes used: these may be either of wooden planks or more informally of lopped tree limbs. Neither is so harsh in appearance as some of the other types of edging, but neither is so long lasting. If planks are used they should be 6 in. × 1 in., and should be buried to half their depth in the soil and secured to stout pegs by means of galvanized nails. The pegs should be 2 ft. long, inserted on the inside of the edgings at intervals of not more than 6 ft.

Patios. Patios are basically places for sitting out in the garden when the weather is fine, and as such are usually paved, either with crazy-paving or formal paving slabs, but there is a wealth of other materials that can be used to provide a variety of surfaces, colours and textures. From a design point of view a patio is a link between the house and the garden, and it should reflect the styles of both.

The method of laying a patio is basically the same as that for a paved drive or path. There must be a firm foundation, and a 2-in. layer of concrete upon which the surface material will be placed. A patio should always be given a slope, so that water will drain away from the house, and a drop of 1 in 60 is sufficient to achieve this, provided that the surface material is laid relatively level. To achieve this drop the patio should be marked out with wooden pegs driven into the ground to the required depth.

Because patios are essentially sun-traps they provide an ideal place for growing tender plants that might not thrive in the open garden. Whether you intend to grow tender plants or not, you will want some colour in the patio, and so beds and borders should be planned before any concrete is laid: so should the position of any tree that is to be grown to cast shade. If the beds are situated at the foot of a wall they need to be at least 18 in. wide, as walls tend to create rain shadows, i.e. places shadowed from rain.

It is not necessary to build a patio on a rectangular plan. They are often made more attractive if a number of differently coloured materials and different textures are used. Areas of sea-washed pebbles set in concrete relieve the monotony of crazy paving, and so do areas of brick laid level with the crazy paving. Garden pools, often with fountains, are frequently incorporated in patios, and the sound of falling water is certainly refreshing on really hot days. Statuary and urns and tubs of flowers all add to the gaiety of a patio.

Fences. Fences are usually, by their very nature, unattractive objects, but they need not remain so. Most types of fencing lend themselves to having plants trained against them. Solid fences are ideal for training roses and other climbing plants against, while mesh fences are ideal for growing twining plants. Ivies, especially the variegated forms, are excellent for covering north-facing fences.

Galvanized wire mesh is probably the least durable fencing material, though it is not as obtrusive as more solid material. Of the longer-lasting types, close-boarded oak fencing is the best but is expensive. Split oak is more durable than sawn oak. Larch, pine, fir and deal are alternatives, but they all need regular treatment with preservatives and, even then will not last so long as oak. Interwoven fencing can be bought in pre-fabricated sections of varying heights and lengths, and is usually supplied with posts and fittings. The panels should be fitted between the posts, not on one side only.

Walls. A well-built brick or stone wall, particularly when it has had time to mellow, is a great asset to a garden but in view of its high costs usually an uneconomic proposition. Fences and hedges usually do just as well in providing privacy or hiding unsightly objects, so the expense can seldom be justified. The average gardener can easily erect a wall up to 3 ft. on his own, but he would be unwise to attempt anything higher unless he is an experienced bricklayer.

Low walls, 2 or 3 ft. high, are often used to mark the boundary across the front of a garden: they are also useful where something permanent is needed to separate a patio from the rest of the garden. Other materials than brick can be used for low walls, and it is very often a good idea to use local, traditional building materials where these occur: among such materials are random stone, flint, both either dressed or not, and sea-washed pebbles in coastal areas.

A type of walling rapidly gaining in popularity is the pierced wall, often known as Italian walling. The effect is more that of a screen than of a solid wall, and in small gardens the lightness and airiness of such pierced walls is much to be preferred to the heaviness of a solid brick wall. Manufacturers now produce pierced wall blocks in a wide variety of patterns.

Hedges. Most gardens benefit from having at least one good length of hedge, whether to provide shelter from cruel winds, privacy, a background to a herbaceous border or quite simply because a good hedge well kept is a joy in itself. The problem with hedges is, of course, that they have to be maintained, but with modern power-driven clippers this is very little trouble. Hedges should always be slightly narrower at the top than at the bottom, and the plants should be planted alternately 10 to 15 in. apart in parallel rows 9 in. apart.

Privet is probably the most ubiquitous of hedging plants. It is cheap, easily raised from cuttings, and relatively fast-growing. It withstands clipping well, does not suffer from winds and will grow in practically any soil and situation. Its disadvantages are that it is apt to lose its leaves in winter, needs clipping at least three times a year, preferably four times, and that it has greedy roots which rob plants growing close to it. Common privet is a dull green, but golden privet is cheerfully bright and is particularly useful for planting in shaded situations. The two can be intermixed, either planted alternately or planted two of golden privet to one of green privet, and hedges of this type are probably more colourful than hedges made of only one or the other type of privet.

Beech makes a more permanent hedge, and is usually recommended where a taller hedge is required. It will make a good hedge up to as much as 8 or 10 ft. It thrives in all soils, including chalk ones, and stands clipping well, normally needing clipping only twice a year. It is valued for the freshness of the green of the new leaves as they appear in spring, and for the russet colouring of its leaves in autumn. These are retained through the winter. Apart from the greenleaved form there is a purple-leaved form, and the well-known copper-beech, with leaves of a rather lighter colour than those of the purple beech. Beech hedges may be composed either of all green-leaved plants or of these intermixed with the coloured-leaf forms. Hedges made entirely of copper or purple beech tend to look rather heavy, but are very striking when used for pleached hedges. Another plant suited to almost all soils is hornbeam, which is often confused with beech: indeed, so like beech is hornbeam that many so-called beech hedges are in fact composed of hornbeam.

Evergreen hedges have the advantage of maintaining privacy throughout the winter months. They may be composed of either broadleaved shrubs such as holly, or of coniferous shrubs such as yew or cupressus. Of the broadleaved evergreens there can be

Oriental poppies and columbines beside a garden seat. An attractive corner like this is essential to every garden. After the hard work one needs somewhere to sit and enjoy the fruits of one's labour.

little doubt but that holly makes the most attractive hedge, particularly if it is allowed to grow tall – say to 12 ft. Such a hedge is practically impenetrable by winds or animals. Moreover, being a European native, it is absolutely hardy in even the coldest areas. The usual objection raised against using holly as a hedge is that the fallen leaves, with their persistent sharp spines, are liable to puncture tender fingers when weeding unsuspectingly in the garden. This is not a serious drawback: there are many forms which have only the terminal spine. The common holly itself has dark, shining green leaves, but there are forms with leaves variegated either gold or white, and these make more colourful hedges. It is not advisable to mix the green and the variegated forms since they have very different rates of growth.

Laurel, though often used, is really only suitable for gardens of the largest size. To look good it needs room to grow, and should be at least 8 ft. tall. Its main problem, apart from the space it requires, is that it needs to be trimmed by hand, each shoot being cut with secateurs: if it is simply cut with shears or with a power-driven tool the leaves that have been cut in half will turn brown and spoil the whole appearance of the hedge. And it has greedy roots: nothing worth while will grow within 10 ft. of a laurel hedge.

Yew makes a particularly attractive formal hedge. It is favoured not because of the slowness of its growth, but because it makes a particularly neat hedge and will stand trimming well. Yew hedges have great longevity, and the same hedge will look just the same in 100 or 200 years as it does today, though that is a consideration that does not concern many people nowadays. It is extremely hardy and will grow on all soils including chalk, and makes an excellent hedge anything from 3 to 20 ft. high. There are few other backgrounds that show off the colourfulness of a herbaceous border better than a well-clipped yew hedge. There are forms with golden leaves, and these look good used either mixed with the green form or on their own. Yew is poisonous to many animals, and this should be borne in mind when planting a yew hedge or disposing of the clippings.

Index

125

0   0
INCH CM
1
2
1   3
4
2   5
6
7
3   8
9
4   10
11
12
5   13
14
15
6   16